LONGMAN

CORNERSTONE

B

Practice Book

Anna Uhl Chamot

Jim Cummins

Sharroky Hollie

PEARSON
Longman

Longman Cornerstone B
Practice Book

Pearson Education, 10 Bank Street, White Plains, NY 10606

Staff credits: The people who made up the *Longman Cornerstone* team, representing editorial, production, design, manufacturing, and marketing, are John Ade, Rhea Banker, Liz Barker, Kenna Bourke, Jeffrey Buckner, Brandon Carda, Daniel Comstock, Martina Deignan, Gina DiLillo, Nancy Flaggman, Cate Foley, Patrice Fraccio, Tracy Grenier, Zach Halper, Henry Hild, Sarah Hughes, Karen Kawaguchi, Lucille Kennedy, Ed Lamprich, Jamie Lawrence, Niki Lee, Christopher Leonowicz, Tara Maceyak, Katrinka Moore, Linda Moser, Liza Pleva, Edie Pullman, Monica Rodriguez, Tara Rose, Tania Saiz-Sousa, Chris Siley, Heather St. Clair, Loretta Steeves, and Andrew Vaccaro.
Text composition: The Quarasan Group, Inc.

ISBN-13: 978-0-13-235692-3
ISBN-10: 0-13-235692-9

PEARSON LONGMAN ON THE **WEB**

Pearsonlongman.com offers online resources for teachers and students. Access our Companion Websites, our online catalog, and our local offices around the world.

Visit us at **www.pearsonlongman.com**.

Printed in the United States of America
16 17 -V016- 16 15 14 13

CONTENTS

UNIT 1

UNIT 2

UNIT 3

CONTENTS

UNIT 4

UNIT 5

UNIT 6

Name _____ Date _____

Vocabulary

Use with Student Book pages 8–9.

Key Words

young
protect
communicates
secure

A. Choose the word that *best* completes each sentence. Write the word.

1. Most animals _____ their babies from danger.

2. Baby wallabies feel warm and _____ in their mother's pouch.

3. Adult animals teach their _____ how to care for themselves.

4. A mother _____ with her babies by making sounds.

B. Choose the word that *best* matches the meaning of the underlined words. Write the word.

5. Shells <u>give a safe place to</u> turtles and snails. _____

6. Birds feed worms to their <u>small babies</u>. _____

7. Baby animals feel <u>safe</u> when their mothers are near.

   _____

8. A bird <u>sends a message</u> to other birds when it sings.

   _____

3

C. Answer the questions.

9. What are some places where animals feel **secure**?

_____

_____

10. How do some animals **protect** their babies?

_____

_____

11. How do you know when a cat **communicates**?

_____

_____

12. What do birds teach their **young** to do?

_____

_____

Academic Words

D. Read each sentence. Write a new sentence using the underlined word.

13. My friends always <u>involve</u> me in their plans.

_____

14. Animals <u>require</u> help from their owners.

_____

 Write a paragraph telling what you know about animals and their young. Share your paragraph with a family member.

Name _____   Date _____

Reader's Companion
Use with Student Book pages 10–19.

Taking Care of the Young

   Raccoon babies are very small when they are born. They cannot stand or open their eyes. Only female raccoons take care of the babies. A mother might have four babies to take care of alone. She must leave them in the den when she looks for food. In the den, the raccoon babies are safe from danger.

   The mother raccoon worries that other animals might find her den. So after a few months, the family moves. By then, the babies can walk and climb. Their mother has taught them to take care of themselves.

Use What You Know
List three things you know about raccoons.

1. _____

2. _____

3. _____

Reading Strategy
MARK the TEXT

What are raccoons like when they are born? Underline one sentence that tells you.

Comprehension Check
MARK the TEXT

Circle the sentences that explain which parent takes care of the raccoon babies.

5

Use the Strategy

Why does the mother raccoon move her family? Reread the passage to find the answer.

_____

_____

_____

Retell It!

Retell this passage. Pretend you are a zookeeper. Tell a group of children about raccoons.

_____

_____

_____

_____

Reader's Response

Which of the animals would you like to learn more about? Why?

_____

_____

_____

Retell the passage to a family member.

Name _____ Date _____

Phonics: Short Vowels

Use with Student Book page 20.

> **A word is likely to have a short vowel sound when:**
> - **it has a single vowel.**
> - **the vowel has a single consonant before and after it.**
>   **CVC**

Circle the words with the CVC pattern. Then write the short vowel sound. The first word is done for you.

1. (pin) _short i_ _____

2. sad _____

3. hot _____

4. food _____

5. wet _____

6. cube _____

7. him _____

8. sky _____

9. bag _____

10. red _____

Brainstorm a list of ten words with the CVC pattern. Share your words with a family member.

7

Comprehension: Reread for Details

Use with Student Book pages 22–23.

Read the passage below. Reread to help answer the questions.

Unusual Horses

Seahorses are unusual animals. You might think a seahorse is a horse that likes to swim. Seahorses do swim! But they don't have legs. They can't even live on land. Seahorses are fish.

Seahorses look different from other fish. A seahorse's head looks a bit like a horse's head. Many seahorses also have tiny fins. And seahorses have a tail that can curl up under them. Seahorses use their tail to hold onto plants, and sometimes each other.

One unusual thing about seahorses is their pouch. Other animals have pouches, too. But among seahorses, the father has the pouch. He keeps the eggs safe until the babies are ready to be born.

1. How do you think the seahorse got its name?

_____

2. What can a seahorse do with its tail?

_____

3. How is a father seahorse different from a mother seahorse?

_____

Share what you learned about seahorses with a family member.

Name _____ Date _____

Grammar: Plural Nouns

Use with Student Book page 24.

> **To show more than one:**
> - **Add -*s* to most nouns.**
> - **Add -*es* to nouns ending in *ch*, *sh*, *s*, *ss*, *x*, and *z*.**
> - **If a noun ends in *y*, change the *y* to *i* and add -*es*.**

A. Write the plural form of each noun.

1. day _____   **4.** bunny _____

2. nose _____   **5.** bus _____

3. car _____   **6.** rock _____

B. Write a sentence using each word.

7. wishes _____

_____

8. faces _____

_____

9. ponies _____

_____

10. bunches _____

_____

Home-School Connection Think of two more examples for each of the rules above. Share your examples with a family member.

9

Spelling: CVC Pattern

Use with Student Book page 25.

A. Fill in the blank with a vowel to make a word with the CVC pattern. Some examples have more than one choice.

1. h _____ t

2. c _____ p

3. p _____ n

4. r _____ g

B. Fill in the blank with a consonant to make a word with the CVC pattern. Some examples have more than one choice.

5. no _____

6. ca _____

7. _____ it

8. _____ an

 Write two sentences. Use a CVC word in each sentence.

_____

_____

Home-School Connection Use the examples above to write three additional CVC words with the short vowel sound. Share your words with a family member.

Name _____ Date _____

Vocabulary

Use with Student Book pages 26–27.

Key Words

unusual
dedicated
executive
capital
museum
memorabilia

A. Choose the word that *best* completes each sentence. Write the word.

1. Many strange and _____ animals have lived at the White House.

2. Washington, D.C., is the

_____ of the United States.

3. Presidents loved their pets and were _____ to them.

4. The White House is the _____ building.

5. Pictures, objects, and other _____ tell about our Presidents' pets.

B. Choose the word that *best* matches the meaning of the underlined words. Write the word.

6. Llamas and hyenas are <u>odd and uncommon</u> pets. _____

7. People study <u>things from long ago</u> to learn about the past.

_____

8. We visited the <u>building with pictures</u> <u>and important objects</u> because

we like art. _____

9. Our President works in our nation's <u>center of government</u>.

_____

10. Most people are <u>caring and loving</u> to their animals. _____

11

C. Answer the questions.

11. What kinds of things can you see in a **museum**?

_____

12. How do people show they are **dedicated** to their pets?

_____

13. What kinds of **memorabilia** can teach about the past?

_____

14. Why is our nation's **capital** important?

_____

15. What animals do you think are the most **unusual**?

_____

16. What happens in the **executive** mansion?

_____

Academic Words

D. Read each sentence. Write a new sentence using the underlined word.

17. Janna can <u>confirm</u> that this is her book.

_____

18. Mr. and Mrs. Toledo <u>reside</u> in your city.

_____

Write two new questions. Each question should contain at least two of the key words. Share your questions with a family member.

Name _____   Date _____

Reader's Companion

Use with Student Book pages 28–31.

The Presidents' Pets

Animals that run, jump, hop, swim, and fly have lived in the Executive Mansion. That is another name for the White House. The President's home in Washington, D.C., is not a zoo. But many exotic pets have lived there.

Calvin Coolidge and his wife had a cat named Tiger. But they also were dedicated to a raccoon named Rebecca. The President often walked this strange pet outside at night.

John Quincy Adams owned an alligator. Teddy Roosevelt had a zebra, a lion, a hyena, and many other pets!

Reading Strategy

Look at the title. List two things this passage could be about.

1. _____

2. _____

Genre

Magazine articles always have a title. List two other titles you could give this passage.

1. _____

2. _____

Comprehension Check   MARK the TEXT

Circle three different kinds of pets that have lived in the White House.

Use the Strategy

Preview the first paragraph of the passage. Explain why the President's home is not a zoo.

_____

_____

_____

Retell It!

Retell the passage. Pretend you are President Coolidge. Write a journal entry about your pet.

_____

_____

_____

_____

Reader's Response

Write about an unusual animal you would like to have. Explain why you would choose that animal as your pet.

_____

_____

_____

Retell the passage to a family member.

Name _____ Date _____

Phonics: Long Vowels with Silent *e*

Use with Student Book page 32.

> These words follow the CVCe pattern. The first vowel in each word has a long vowel sound. The second vowel—the letter *e*—is silent.

a_e	e_e	i_e	o_e	u_e
game	Pete	hide	tone	rule

A. Unscramble the letters to write a CVCe word.

1. e s n o _____

3. n t e u _____

2. c a e f _____

4. i e r c _____

B. Choose one vowel that will complete both words in the row. Write the vowel.

CVC Words	CVCe Words
5. m _____ d	m _____ de
6. t _____ b	t _____ be
7. h _____ p	h _____ pe
8. h _____ d	h _____ de

Home-School Connection Think of another pair of words that follow the CVC and CVCe pattern shown in the chart above. Share them with a family member.

Comprehension: Preview

Use with Student Book pages 34–35.

Read the title and answer the first question. Then read the passage and answer the second question.

The Unusual House Guest

When Melinda came home, her bedroom was a mess. The window and closet door were open. Her clothes were everywhere. "Mom," said Melinda, "Tilly has been in my room." Tilly was Melinda's younger sister. Sometimes Tilly liked to wear her older sister's clothes. But it wasn't Tilly. Melinda picked up her clothes from the floor. Then she heard a sound. "Aaaah!" she screamed. "Mom, there's an animal in my closet!"

1. What did you learn about the story from the title?

_____

_____

_____

_____

2. What do you predict will happen next?

_____

_____

_____

_____

 **Tell a family member about how well you were able to predict what the story was about.**

Name _____   Date _____

Grammar: Common Nouns and Proper Nouns

Use with Student Book page 36.

A. Write two proper nouns for each common noun. The first row is done for you.

Common Nouns	Proper Nouns
1. state	Maine, New Mexico
2. person	
3. ocean	
4. country	
5. river	

B. Rewrite each sentence. Begin each proper noun with a capital letter.

6. I saw governor thompson, his wife, and their son john last friday.

_____

7. The election day party was on tuesday night at the library.

_____

8. My aunt and miss goldberg are teachers at memorial school.

_____

 Write a short paragraph that includes ten different proper nouns. Share your paragraph with a family member.

17

Spelling: CVCe Pattern

Use with Student Book page 37.

SPELLING TIP

Notice that the word **home** has the CVCe pattern. Remember to use the CVCe pattern when you write.

A. Fill in the blank with a vowel to make a CVCe word.

1. My mother likes to b _____ ke.

2. Yesterday she m _____ de us cookies.

3. I h _____ pe she cooks us something today.

4. It takes a lot of t _____ me to cook.

B. Read each clue. Fill in the blank to complete the CVCe word.

5. you do it with your hands   w _____ ve

6. you live in it   h _____ me

7. you play it   g _____ me

8. you stand in it   l _____ ne

 Write about something you did this week at home or at school. Use three CVCe words.

_____

_____

_____

_____

 **Work with a family member to practice spelling the words you wrote above.**

Name _____ Date _____

Vocabulary
Use with Student Book pages 38–39.

Key Words

- shimmer
- frisky
- glowed
- warm
- breath
- companion

A. Choose the word that *best* completes each sentence. Write the word.

1. He saw a star _____ in the sky.

2. The campfire kept us _____ during the cold night.

3. A small light _____ in the darkness.

4. The _____ animals jumped and rolled through the tall grass.

5. I ran until I was out of _____.

6. A pet can be a person's best _____.

B. Choose the word that *best* matches the meaning of the underlined words. Write the word.

7. The moon gave off a soft light. _____

8. I felt a little hot under the heavy blanket. _____

9. My pet is my favorite friend and playmate. _____

10. Divers hold their air in their lungs. _____

11. At night, lights shine softly on the water. _____

12. Puppies are lively and playful. _____

19

C. Answer the questions.

13. What do **frisky** animals do?

_____

14. How do you stay **warm** in cold weather?

_____

15. Why is it nice to have a **companion**?

_____

16. What kinds of things **shimmer**?

_____

17. What does your **breath** look like in cold weather?

_____

18. What **glowed** in the sky yesterday?

_____

Academic Words

D. Read each sentence. Write a new sentence using the underlined word.

19. Bobby is my <u>partner</u> on the school project.

_____

20. I feel a special <u>bond</u> with my friend Suzanne.

_____

Use each key word in a sentence. Share your sentences with a family member.

Name _____ Date _____

Reader's Companion

Use with Student Book pages 40–45.

The Star Llama

The star llama drank for a very long time. Then she looked at the sad Inca boy and smiled. When she jumped back into the sky, bits of llama wool fell. The boy felt the silver wool. It was soft and warm.

As the sun began to rise, the boy gathered the llama wool. It glowed in his hands like starlight. He carried the wool to the city and sold it. With the money, he bought a house and two frisky young llamas. He never forgot the star llama. And he was never lonely again.

Genre

In fables, animals often behave like humans. Underline a sentence that describes the llama acting like a human.

Reading Strategy

List two things that are fantasy.

1. _____

2. _____

Comprehension Check

Draw a box around one sentence that is reality.

Use the Strategy

What happened when the llama jumped into the sky? Reread the passage to find the answer. Tell if the answer is fantasy or reality.

_____

_____

_____

Retell It!

Retell this passage. Pretend you are a storyteller visiting a class of first graders.

_____

_____

_____

_____

Reader's Response

What did you learn about the boy from the passage?

_____

_____

_____

Retell the passage to a family member.

Name _____ Date _____

Word Analysis: Endings -s, -es, -ed

Use with Student Book page 46.

> Add -ed to a word when you want to show something that happened in the past. Add -s or -es to a word when you want to show something that is happening now.

Put a check in the boxes that tell about each word when -ed is added. The first one is done for you.

	-ed sounds like d	-ed sounds like t	-ed adds a syllable
1. walked	☐	✓	☐
2. planted	☐	☐	☐
3. filled	☐	☐	☐
4. rushed	☐	☐	☐

5. Write a sentence to tell what a friend does every day. Use one word ending in -s.

_____

6. Write a sentence to tell what a friend did yesterday. Use one word ending in -ed.

_____

Write two sentences to tell what you did on your last birthday. Use words with the -ed ending. Share your sentences with a family member.

Comprehension: Fantasy and Reality

Use with Student Book pages 48–49.

Read each statement. Do you think it is possible? Write R for Reality and F for Fantasy.

1. A duck lays one thousand eggs in a day. _____

2. The dog used different sounds to communicate. _____

3. His cat ran as fast as the car. _____

4. Scientists discovered a fish living in a tree. _____

5. New kinds of animals come to Earth from outer space. _____

6. Her pet goldfish lived for three years. _____

7. The stars are home to many animals. _____

8. The seagull lost a feather. _____

Home-School Connection Tell a family member one event that could be reality and one event that would have to be fantasy.

Name _____ Date _____

Grammar: Subject and Object Pronouns

Use with Student Book page 50.

Subject Pronouns	I	you	he	she	it	we	they
Object Pronouns	me	you	him	her	it	us	them

A. Choose a pronoun to complete each sentence. Some examples have more than one choice.

1. Do _____ know what time the zoo opens?

2. Can you give _____ a ride there?

3. I will sit with _____ in the back seat.

4. The penguins always make _____ laugh.

B. Read each sentence. Underline the subject pronouns. Draw a box around the object pronouns.

5. I brought him to see the lions.

6. We thought they looked hungry.

7. He told him they were just tired.

8. Can they take me to see the whales next?

Write two sentences that each contain both a subject and an object pronoun. Share your sentences with a family member.

25

Spelling: Endings -s, -es, -ed

Use with Student Book page 51.

A. Add -s or -es to write the correct present-tense form of each verb.

1. ask _____

2. push _____

3. hand _____

4. clap _____

5. watch _____

B. Use the correct past tense verb to complete each sentence.

6. We ran when the bear _____. (growl)

7. My pet skunk _____ living in the garage. (like)

8. He _____ the dishes after dinner. (wash)

9. She _____ with her friend every day. (play)

10. The boys _____ into the pond. (jump)

 Write about an experience you had with an animal. Use three words used as answers on this page.

_____

_____

_____

 Write sentences using both the present and past tenses for two of the words. Share your sentences with a family member.

Name _____   Date _____

Review

Use with Student Book pages 2–51.

A. Answer the questions after reading Unit 1. You can go back and reread to help find the answers.

1. Which of the following questions is NOT answered by the end of *Taking Care of the Young*? Circle the letter of the correct answer.
   a. Do male emperor penguins take care of their babies?
   b. Do adult swans keep animals away from their cygnets?
   c. Where does the father raccoon find food for his babies?
   d. Do older joeys sometimes leave their mother's pouch?

2. How does a clown fish protect its eggs?

   _____

3. Read this sentence from the selection.

   > Mother wallabies have an unusual way to protect their babies.

   What does *protect* mean?
   a. watch   **c.** hurt
   b. trouble   **d.** keep safe

4. Read this sentence from *The Presidents' Pets*. Then underline the proper nouns.

   > The museum has a statue of Fala, Franklin Delano Roosevelt's terrier.

5. Write a sentence about Pauline, the cow that lived at the White House.

   _____

6. Which word does NOT have the CVCe pattern? Circle the letter of the correct answer.
   a. home   **b.** cat   **c.** make   **d.** like

7. Read these sentences from the story.

Presidential pets from coyotes to owls have lived in the White House. The White House has been home to some unusual pets!

What does **unusual** mean?
a. ordinary
b. different
c. happy
d. fun

8. What did the boy in *The Star Llama* do with the wool that fell from the sky?

_____

_____

_____

B. Read these sentences from *The Star Llama*. Then answer questions 9 and 10.

The boy cried for a very long time. But there was no one to comfort him. One star began to shimmer. Slowly, the star took the shape of the old llama. When she jumped back into the sky, bits of llama wool fell.

9. Circle one subject pronoun.

10. Find one sentence that tells the reader the story is a fantasy. Then find one sentence that tells about something that could happen in real life. Write each sentence in the correct column.

Fantasy	Reality

Tell a family member something new you learned in this unit.

Name _____ Date _____

Vocabulary

Use with Student Book pages 64–65.

Key Words

- volcano
- ash
- lava
- crater
- eruption

A. Choose the word that *best* completes each sentence. Write the word.

1. The _____ in the air made it hard to breathe.

2. It is a bad idea to live on a _____.

3. The largest _____ on the moon is over 1,300 miles across.

4. Hot _____ poured down the side of the volcano.

5. The loud _____ hurt my ears.

B. Choose the word that *best* matches the meaning of the underlined words. Write the word.

6. _____ The <u>exploding smoke, fire, and rocks</u> made a lot of noise.

7. _____ Martin explored the <u>round hole in the ground</u>.

8. _____ Dad says to stay away from the <u>mountain with a hole in the top</u>.

9. _____ <u>Hot liquid</u> comes out of volcanoes.

10. _____ The logs in our campfire will turn to <u>soft gray powder</u>.

C. Answer the questions.

11. When should you stay away from a **volcano**?

_____

12. How can you avoid walking into a **crater**?

_____

13. Why is it a bad idea to touch **lava**?

_____

14. What is the loudest **eruption** you have heard?

_____

15. Where do you see **ash**?

_____

Academic Words

D. Read each sentence. Write a new sentence using the underlined word.

16. The two houses are <u>similar</u> in size.

_____

17. There is no <u>evidence</u> of life on other planets.

_____

 Write a question using each key word. Ask a family member to answer your questions.

Name _____ Date _____

Reader's Companion

Use with Student Book pages 66–71.

Vesuvius Erupts!

About 2,000 people stayed in the city. Some chose to stay. Others were trapped. All of them died. But 20,000 people were able to escape.

In less than two days, ash and rocks buried the city. Heavy rain made the ash hard like cement. Pompeii stayed buried for almost 1,700 years!

In about 1750, the King of Naples ordered workers to uncover Pompeii.

Use What You Know

List three things you know about volcanoes.

1. _____

2. _____

3. _____

Genre

Underline one sentence that tells you *Vesuvius Erupts!* is a narrative text.

Reading Strategy

Circle the sentence that tells what happened almost 1,700 years after Pompeii was buried.

31

Use the Strategy

How did making predictions help you to understand the passage?

_____

_____

_____

Retell It!

Retell this passage. Pretend you are a news reporter living in Pompeii at the time of the eruption.

_____

_____

_____

_____

Reader's Response

Think about Pompeii at the time Vesuvius erupts. What would you do to stay safe?

_____

_____

_____

Retell the passage to a family member.

Name _____ Date _____

Word Analysis: Ending -ed

Use with Student Book page 72.

> Writers add **-ed** to a regular verb to show
> something happened in the past.

**Check the boxes that tell about each word when -ed is added.
The first one is done for you.**

	-ed sounds like d	-ed sounds like t	-ed adds a syllable
1. melted	√	☐	√
2. jumped	☐	☐	☐
3. called	☐	☐	☐
4. wanted	☐	☐	☐
5. looked	☐	☐	☐
6. barked	☐	☐	☐
7. tasted	☐	☐	☐
8. pulled	☐	☐	☐
9. needed	☐	☐	☐
10. missed	☐	☐	☐

Home-School Connection Write sentences in the past tense using three of the words above.
Share your sentences with a family member.

Comprehension: Sequence of Events

Use with Student Book pages 74–75.

Read the passage.

Jose's Afternoon

It was a sunny afternoon. Jose sat at his desk. He looked up at the clock. The clock said it was two o'clock. School would soon be over. Jose wanted to be outside. Suddenly, the bell rang. Jose ran out of school. He saw his friends. Together they ran to the park. They played soccer for an hour. Jose scored a goal. His team won the game. After the game, Jose walked home.

List the story events in the correct sequence. Write 1, 2, 3, 4, and 5 on the lines.

_____ He saw that school was almost over.

_____ His team won the game.

_____ Jose played soccer for an hour.

_____ The school bell rang.

_____ Jose sat at his desk and looked at the clock.

 **Write three sentences that tell what Jose did next. Share your sentences with a family member.**

Name _____ Date _____

Grammar: Action Verbs

Use with Student Book page 76.

> **Action verbs** describe what the subject of a sentence does or did.

A. Read each sentence. Underline the action verb.

1. The kids walked to the park.

2. They played a game of softball.

3. The rain fell from the sky.

4. The kids moved to a dry place.

5. It rained for a long time.

B. Write your own sentences using the action verbs.

6. called

_____

7. jumped

_____

8. pushed

_____

Write sentences using more action verbs. Share them with a family member.

Spelling: Past Tense Words with -*ed*

Use with Student Book page 77.

Read each sentence. Use -*ed* to rewrite each verb in the past tense.

1. My dogs bark in the morning.

_____

2. Snow covers her doghouse.

_____

3. My brother and I watch the TV news.

_____

4. We wait for the weather report. _____

5. We play outside in the snow. _____

6. We like our snowman. _____

SPELLING TIP

Regular verbs that tell about actions in the past end in -*ed*. Make sure you add -*ed* to regular verbs when you write about the past.

 Write about a snowy day. Tell what the kids did when the snow ended.

_____

_____

_____

_____

 **Write a sentence for each of the spelling words. Show a family member how to pronounce the words.**

Name _____ Date _____

Vocabulary

Use with Student Book pages 78–79.

Key Words

breeze
hurricane
shelter
lightning
thunder

A. Choose the word that *best* matches the meaning of the underlined words. Write the word.

1. The <u>storm with heavy wind and rain</u> pulled street signs from the ground. _____

2. We saw <u>flashes of light in the sky</u> during the storm.

   _____

3. Your house is a good <u>safe place</u> when it rains.

   _____

4. Did you feel the <u>soft wind</u> on your face? _____

5. The <u>loud noise in the clouds</u> sounded like a train.

   _____

B. Read each clue. Find the key word in the row of letters. Then circle the word.

6. spark of light in the sky   o n e l i g h t n i n g t u r n s h

7. gently moving air   d e r b r e e z e f h s t h u i r k

8. large, dangerous storm   o d h u r r i c a n e o o n i n g q

9. protected spot   z e r r f i s h e l t e r m s i t w

10. noise in sky during some storms   u r c z d t h u n d e r e e z e h l

C. Answer the questions.

11. Why should people leave the shore during a **hurricane**?

_____

12. What does it mean when you hear **thunder**?

_____

13. Why is it important to find **shelter** during a storm?

_____

14. Why is **lightning** dangerous?

_____

15. Can a **breeze** make a tree fall down?

_____

Academic Words

D. Read each sentence. Write a new sentence using the underlined word.

16. A <u>major</u> thunderstorm destroyed my garden.

_____

17. We live in a <u>region</u> that has many mountains.

_____

 **Use each of the vocabulary words in a sentence. Share your sentences with a family member.**

Name _____ Date _____

Reader's Companion

Use with Student Book pages 80–85.

Hurricane!

A man ran toward us. He worked at a nearby hotel.

"Señor! Señorita!" he called. "A big storm is coming. You must leave the beach now!" He told us that a hurricane was approaching. Everyone had to go to a shelter.

"But the water is so nice," I said sadly.

"Hurricanes are dangerous. We must leave," Dad said.

Mom smiled to make me feel better. Just then, I felt a breeze. Suddenly, the wind grew stronger. Sand flew into my face.

"Let's go!" Dad said.

Use What You Know

List three things you know about hurricanes.

1. _____

2. _____

3. _____

Reading Strategy

MARK the TEXT

Circle two examples in the passage that tell you about the setting.

Comprehension Check

MARK the TEXT

Someone ran over to the family on the beach. Underline the paragraph that tells you who this was.

Use the Strategy

What clues in the passage helped you understand what a hurricane is like?

_____

_____

_____

_____

Retell It!

Retell this passage. Pretend you are a weather reporter. Tell people about the approaching hurricane.

_____

_____

_____

_____

Reader's Response

What would you do if a hurricane were coming?

_____

_____

_____

_____

Home-School Connection   Retell the passage to a family member.

40

Name _____ Date _____

Phonics: Digraphs *ch, sh, th*

Use with Student Book page 86.

> The letter pairs **ch, sh,** and **th** each have one sound.
> These letters can be anywhere in a word.

**Read each word. Write the word in the correct column of the chart.
The first one is done for you.**

beaches	catch	~~chair~~
fishing	mother	shore
three	wash	with

Letters	Beginning	Middle	End
ch	1. _chair_	2. _____	3. _____
sh	4. _____	5. _____	6. _____
th	7. _____	8. _____	9. _____

Home-School Connection Think of one word to add to each box in the chart. Show your words to a family member.

Comprehension: Clues to Setting

Use with Student Book pages 88–89.

Read each story. Then answer the questions.

1. It was summer. The sand was very hot. The waves were tall. The breeze smelled salty. "Do you think the water is warm?" Jerry asked his friend. Caleb laughed. "There's only one way to find out."

Write two clues that tell where the story takes place.

_____

_____

Where are Jerry and Caleb?

_____

2. "There's nowhere to park," said Dad. Joanie looked around. The parking lot was filled with cars. "Look at all these shoppers," said Joanie. It was a rainy Saturday. People wanted to be inside. Joanie sighed. Dad said, "After we find a place to park, we'll go to your favorite stores."

Write two clues that tell where the story takes place.

_____

_____

Where are Dad and Joanie?

_____

 **Home-School Connection** Tell a family member about a storm you experienced, read about, or saw in a film. Include details about the setting.

Name _____ Date _____

Grammar: Adjectives and Noun Phrases

Use with Student Book page 90.

> **Nouns** name people, places, or things.
> **Adjectives** describe nouns.
> Adjectives and nouns work together to form a **noun phrase**.

A. Draw a line between each adjective and a noun. Then write the noun phrase. The first one is done for you.

Adjective	Noun	
1. soft	wind	_soft pillow_
2. green	building	_____
3. cold	pillow	_____
4. tall	nail	_____
5. sharp	grass	_____

B. Write the noun phrase in each sentence.

6. The thunder is loud. _____

7. The ground was hard. _____

8. The students were funny. _____

9. The food was hot. _____

10. The games are difficult. _____

 **Make sentences using five of the noun phrases. Show your sentences to a family member.**

43

Spelling: /k/ Sound

Use with Student Book page 91.

Underline the word in each sentence that has the /k/ sound. Draw a box around the letter or letters that spell the /k/ sound. Then write the word.

1. Books are nice to read.

_____

2. Did you pick the flowers? _____

3. Would you like to play? _____

4. The water was as cold as ice. _____

Write a short story about a black cat that acts like a kangaroo.

_____

_____

_____

Think of two words for each /k/ sound spelled with *c*, *k*, and *ck*. Use each word in a sentence. Share your sentences with a family member.

Name _____ Date _____

Vocabulary
Use with Student Book pages 92–93.

Key Words

bolt
electricity
temperature
evaporate

A. Choose the word that *best* completes each sentence. Write the word.

1. A _____ of lightning

   hit the tree.

2. Computers and TV sets need _____ to work.

3. Water will _____ before it turns into gas.

4. We were very cold because the _____ was low.

B. Read each sentence. Write TRUE or FALSE.

5. A bicycle needs **electricity** to work. _____

6. When the **temperature** is high, many people go to the beach.

   _____

7. A bolt of **lightning** can be dangerous. _____

8. Water will not **evaporate** if it boils. _____

C. **Answer the questions.**

9. What does a **bolt** of lightning look like?

_____

10. How does **electricity** make your life easier?

_____

11. What is the **temperature** like in winter?

_____

12. How can you make water **evaporate**?

_____

Academic Words

D. **Read each sentence. Write a new sentence using the underlined word.**

13. Cords <u>conduct</u> the electricity needed to power machines.

_____

14. Parents give their children <u>security</u> and love.

_____

 Write a clue for each key word. Ask a family member to guess the answer.

Name _____   Date _____

Reader's Companion

Use with Student Book pages 94–97.

Thunder and Lightning

Staying Safe in a Lightning Storm

1. Check if thunderstorms are in the forecast.

2. Find shelter in a strong building or in a car with a hard roof.

3. Do not stand under trees that are alone in the middle of a field. Do not stand under tall trees when there are shorter trees close by.

4. Do not stand near things that are made of metal.

Use What You Know

List three things you know about thunderstorms.

1. _____

2. _____

3. _____

Reading Strategy

How do you know that this is an example of a how-to poster? Circle one feature of a how-to poster.

Comprehension Check

List three good places to put this poster.

1. _____

2. _____

3. _____

47

Use the Strategy

Where else have you seen a how-to poster? What did the poster teach or tell you to do?

_____

_____

_____

_____

Retell It!

Retell this passage. Pretend you were caught in a thunderstorm. Tell how you followed these rules to stay safe.

_____

_____

_____

_____

Reader's Response

Write a list of safety rules to follow during a hurricane. Use what you read in the passage as a model.

_____

_____

_____

 **Retell the passage to a family member.**

Name _____ Date _____

Word Analysis: Word Parts

Use with Student Book page 98.

> Little words can be part of bigger words. Some bigger words are made of two little words put together.

A. Write the smaller word found in each word.

1. lightning _____

2. faster _____

3. unwelcome _____

4. playing _____

5. teacher _____

B. Read each word. Add another word or a word part to make a larger word.

6. some _____

7. talk _____

8. fun _____

9. light _____

10. good _____

Make as many words as possible from the word *day* by adding words or word parts. Share your list with a family member.

Comprehension: Compare Genres

Use with Student Book pages 100–101.

Read each passage. Mark an X next to the correct genre. Explain the features that helped you to decide.

1. Dear Aunt Peggy,

How are you? I am fine. Space Camp is fun! Every day I learn something new. Maybe some day I will visit the Space Station.

Love, Bobbie

_____ Informational Article

_____ How-To Poster

_____ Letter

_____

_____

2. Benjamin Franklin was a scientist. He learned about electricity. He also was a great leader. Franklin helped write the Declaration of Independence. He also helped start the first public library. Today, Americans thank Benjamin Franklin for his work in science, politics, and literature.

_____ Informational Article

_____ How-To Poster

_____ Letter

_____

_____

Home-School Connection Write a short letter to a friend. Explain to a family member why your letter is different from an informational article and a how-to poster.

Name _____ Date _____

Grammar: Commands

Use with Student Book page 102.

> A **command** is a statement that tells a person or a group what to do or how to act.

A. Underline the sentences that are commands.

1. Get the phone!

2. Did you hear the phone ring?

3. Stephan, answer the phone.

4. Call me.

5. You have a new dog!

B. Rewrite each sentence to make a command. The first one is done for you.

6. You want someone to put the book on the table.

   Put the book on the table.
   _____

7. You want your friend to give you that pencil.

   _____

8. You want Maria to hang the clothes in the closet.

   _____

 **Home-School Connection** Write five commands that a school bus driver might use while working. Show your commands to a family member.

51

Spelling: Words Parts

Use with Student Book page 103.

A. Draw a line between each word in
Column A and a word or word part
in Column B to make a new word.
Then write the new word on the line.

		Column A	Column B
1.	_____	quick	body
2.	_____	out	ly
3.	_____	some	y
4.	_____	cloud	side

B. Complete each word using a word part.

ing	un	under	yard

5. build _____   **7.** back _____

6. _____ ground   **8.** _____ tie

  Write a sentence using one of the answer words.

_____

 Use each of the word parts to write another word. Show your words to
a family member.

Name _____ Date _____

Review

Use with Student Book pages 58–103.

A. Answer the questions after reading Unit 2. You can go back and reread to help find the answers.

1. Which question is not answered by the end of *Vesuvius Erupts!*? Circle the letter of the correct answer.

   a. Why did the King of Naples have workers uncover Pompeii?
   b. What fell from the sky after Mt. Vesuvius erupted?
   c. How long did Pompeii stay buried under ash?
   d. What caused the city of Pompeii to disappear?

2. Read these sentences from the story.

   > Boom! Suddenly, the top of Mount Vesuvius blew off! Now the mountain had a crater.

   What does *crater* mean? Circle the letter of the correct answer.

   a. top   c. explode
   b. hole   d. lava

3. Write a sentence telling what Pompeii was like after the eruption of Mt. Vesuvius.

   _____

   _____

4. Underline two words that tell you about the setting at the beginning of *Hurricane!*

   > On our second day of vacation, I splashed in the sea. Mom and Dad sat on the shore. A strong breeze blew sand into my face.

53

5. Write a noun phrase using the noun and the adjective in this sentence.

> The waves were strong that day.

_____

6. Circle the sentence that contains the action verb.

   a. The sky was dark.   **c.** "Our vacation is ruined."

   b. Rain fell from the sky.   **d.** It was the afternoon.

B. Read this passage from _Thunder and Lightning._ **Then answer questions 7–9.**

> Lightning is a big flash of electricity. It is released during a storm. Thunder is the noise we hear when the air explodes.

7. Which word has the digraph _sh?_ _____

8. Identify the genre of the passage.

   a. friendly letter   **b.** how-to poster   **c.** informational article

9. Look at the Venn diagram. Circle the sentence that is incorrect.

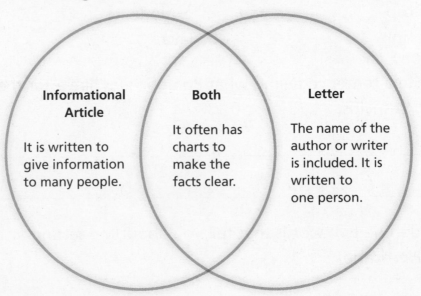

Informational Article

It is written to give information to many people.

Both

It often has charts to make the facts clear.

Letter

The name of the author or writer is included. It is written to one person.

Home-School Connection

Tell a family member something new you learned from this unit.

Name _____ Date _____

Vocabulary

Use with Student Book pages 114–115.

A. **Choose the word that *best* completes each sentence. Write the word.**

1. There are millions of animal

   _____ living in the world.

2. An _____ animal can no longer be found on Earth.

3. The footprints of ancient animals are found in

   _____ .

4. Marble and _____ are types of rocks.

5. We study _____ fossils in science class.

6. Our _____ are body parts that help us lift things.

B. **Read the pairs of sentences. One sentence makes sense. The other is silly. Put a line through the sentence that is silly.**

7. Extinct animals will soon be back.
   Extinct animals are gone forever.

8. You can find fossils underground.
   You can find fossils in the sky.

9. Muscles help us dream.
   Muscles help us move.

10. Many different animal species live in your state.
    Only one animal species lives in your state.

C. Answer the questions.

11. What does a **dinosaur** look like?

_____

12. What **muscles** do you use when you play?

_____

13. What can you learn from **fossils**?

_____

14. Can a fossil be found in **sandstone**?

_____

15. Are a fish and a tree the same **species**?

_____

16. Why do you think some animals become **extinct**?

_____

D. Read each question. Write a response using the underlined word.

17. What missing item have you helped someone <u>locate</u>?

_____

18. Why are fossils a <u>link</u> to our past?

_____

 Write one silly sentence and one sentence that makes sense for the words _dinosaur_ and _sandstone_. Show your sentences to a family member.

Name _____ Date _____

Reader's Companion
Use with Student Book pages 116–119.

My Museum Friend

Resting in sandstone,
Fossils all around.
Bones nestled in old rock.
My species once roamed the ground.

Wondering about my muscles?
Or my powerful legs that are so strong?
I was Dinosaur, king of all the land.
How did everything go wrong?

Extinct! That's what I am to you.
My whole world went haywire.
Like a puff of smoke I disappeared
Because of ice, an asteroid, or fire.

Use the Strategy

What words helped you learn more about the character in the passage?

_____

_____

_____

Retell It!

Retell this passage. Pretend you are a science teacher giving a lesson on dinosaurs.

_____

_____

_____

_____

Reader's Response

Pretend you lived when dinosaurs were alive. What do you think Earth was like then?

_____

_____

_____

Retell the passage to a family member.

Name _____ Date _____

Word Analysis: Synonyms and Antonyms
Use with Student Book page 120.

> **Synonyms** are words that mean the same or almost the same thing.
>
> **Antonyms** are words that have opposite meanings.

A. Write the synonym for each underlined word.

| jump | loud | laugh | shut | seats |

1. The crowd was very <u>noisy</u>. _____

2. All of the <u>chairs</u> were lined up in a row. _____

3. Frogs and rabbits can <u>hop</u>. _____

4. I'll <u>close</u> the window if it gets too hot. _____

5. Funny movies make me <u>giggle</u>. _____

B. Match each word with its antonym. Write the letter of the correct answer.

6. end   _____   **a.** sad

7. freezing _____   **b.** far

8. happy   _____   **c.** begin

9. near   _____   **d.** long

10. short   _____   **e.** boiling

 Think of three synonym pairs and three antonym pairs. Use each word in a sentence. Show your sentences to a family member.

Comprehension: Character

Use with Student Book pages 122–123.

Read the passage. Look for clues that tell you about the character.

I Don't Want to Be Extinct!

The jungle where I live
May be gone one day.
It is getting very small.

I'm a gorilla from Africa.
I eat plants and leaves and ants.
I'm very big. I'm six feet tall.

And I am asking you
My caring human friend
To help to save us all.

1. Where does the main character live? _____

_____

2. What does the main character look like? _____

_____

3. What does the main character eat? _____

_____

4. What does the main character want? _____

_____

 **Write three sentences about an interesting character in a book you read. Show your sentences to a family member.**

Name _____   Date _____

Grammar: Regular Past Tense Verbs

Use with Student Book page 124.

> **Past tense verbs** name actions that already happened.

A. Write the past tense form of each verb shown in parentheses.

1. Yesterday we _____ for the big test.
(study)

2. Last week, she _____ me a pie for dessert.
(bake)

3. My dog _____ his tail when I gave him a bone.
(wag)

4. Two people _____ on the phone.
(talk)

5. Have you ever _____ on ice?
(slip)

B. Circle the correct past tense form of the verb in each sentence.

6. try   Alfred (tried / tryed) to draw a picture.

7. wonder   Peter (wonderd / wondered) if the store was closed.

8. name   They (namd / named) their new baby Emma.

9. hurry   Everyone (hurried / hurreed) to be first on line.

10. tap   He (tapped / taped) me on the shoulder.

Home-School Connection Write three sentences telling what you did yesterday. Use three past tense words. Show your sentences to a family member.

Spelling: Digraphs *ch*, *sh*, *th*

Use with Student Book page 125.

A. Write the word that has a consonant digraph. Then underline the digraph.

> **SPELLING TIP**
>
> The letter pairs *ch*, *sh*, and *th* all say one sound. These pairs can appear anywhere in a word.

1. We ate lunch in the park.

_____

2. Should I meet you after class?

_____

3. My favorite subject is math. _____

4. I like crunchy peanut butter. _____

B. Write *ch*, *sh*, or *th* to make a word. Then write the word.

5. _____ _____ o o s e   _____

6. f i _____ _____   _____

7. _____ _____ a n k   _____

8. r i _____ _____   _____

 Use two of the answer words to write about a visit to a friend.

_____

_____

Home-School Connection Write two words for each of the consonant digraphs. Show your words to a family member.

Name _____ Date _____

Vocabulary
Use with Student Book pages 126–127.

A. Choose the word that *best* completes each sentence. Write the word.

1. When you act silly, everything you

   say is _____!

2. It is everybody's _____ to obey the law.

3. The government _____ meets in Town Hall every Monday.

4. You will get in trouble if you make _____.

5. Julie was _____ with her good grades.

6. We have an interesting _____ of news to tell you.

B. Match each word with its definition. Write the letter of the correct answer.

7. satisfied _____   **a.** a small piece of something

8. duty _____   **b.** something you have to do

9. council _____   **c.** happy with how things are

10. nonsense _____   **d.** something that is silly

11. tidbit _____   **e.** group of leaders

Define each key word in your own words. Show your definitions to a family member.

63

C. Answer the questions.

12. How do you feel when someone makes **mischief**?

_____

13. What do you say when you hear **nonsense**?

_____

14. When was the last time you felt **satisfied**?

_____

15. Why do people in a **council** meet?

_____

16. Where might you learn a **tidbit** of news?

_____

17. What is a **duty** you have at home?

_____

D. Read each question. Write a response using the underlined word.

18. What do people say when they <u>emerge</u> after hiding?

_____

19. What important lesson would you like to <u>transmit</u> to a younger person?

_____

 **Think of another question for each key word. Share your questions with a family member.**

64

Name _____   Date _____

Reader's Companion

Use with Student Book pages 128–133.

Why Mosquitoes Buzz in People's Ears

Just then, Turtle walked by.

"Turtle!" Lion roared. "Are you Snake's friend?"

"What?" Turtle removed the leaves from her ears. "Yes, I am Snake's friend."

"Then why didn't you speak when Snake said hello?" asked Lion.

"I did not hear him," said Turtle. "Mosquito gossips, so I put leaves in my ears."

"All this mischief started with you, Mosquito," the angry lion said. "You may never talk again."

All the animals were satisfied, but not Mosquito. Even today mosquitoes want to talk. But all they can do is buzzzzz!

Use What You Know

List three reasons it's a bad idea to gossip.

1. _____

2. _____

3. _____

Genre

Underline the sentences that tell you this is a pourquoi tale.

Reading Strategy

Lion asked Turtle a question. Circle the sentence that tells what Turtle did next.

Use the Strategy

The passage was written in the order in which the events happened. How did paying attention to the sequence of events help you understand the passage?

_____

_____

_____

Retell It!

Retell this passage. Pretend you are one of the characters in the tale.

_____

_____

_____

_____

Reader's Response

What did this passage teach you about gossip?

_____

_____

_____

Home-School Connection   **Retell the passage to a family member.**

Name _____ Date _____

Phonics: Long Vowel Pairs

Use with Student Book page 134.

> Two vowels together are a **vowel pair**. Usually,
> the first vowel in the pair has a long vowel sound.
> The sound of the second vowel is usually silent.

Long *a*	Long *e*	Long *i*	Long *o*	Long *u*
f<u>ai</u>l, b<u>ay</u>	n<u>ee</u>d	sk<u>ie</u>s	r<u>oa</u>d, f<u>oe</u>	cl<u>ue</u>, s<u>ui</u>t

A. Write the vowel sound in each word. Then circle the letters
that spell that sound. The first one is done for you.

1. d(a)y _____ long a _____

2. g o e s _____

3. b l u e _____

4. f e e t _____

5. t i e d _____

6. l o a f _____

7. r a i n _____

8. f r u i t _____

B. Read each clue. Use a vowel pair to make a word with a long
vowel sound.

9. it sails on water   b _____ _____ t

10. a month of the year   M _____ _____

11. can hold things together   g l _____ _____

12. they are baked with apples   p _____ _____ s

Write another word for each vowel pair in the chart. Show your words to a
family member.

Comprehension: Sequence of Events

Use with Student Book pages 136–137.

Read the passage. Then number the events in the order in which they occurred in the passage. The first one is done for you.

Irving

Irving was a snail. He was growing too big for his little shell. One morning he decided to find a new home.

On the street, Irving saw a small can. He climbed inside. "This house is too big!" he thought.

The next day, Irving found a teacup. "This home looks perfect," he thought. But the teacup had a big crack. "If it rains, I will get wet."

On the third day, Irving saw a store. "I can't find a home. But maybe I can buy one," he thought. Irving crossed the street. "Do you sell homes?" he asked the store owner.

The store owner smiled. "We sell shells," he said.

_____ Irving climbed inside a small can.

_____ Irving saw a store.

___1___ Irving was too big for his shell.

_____ The store owner said he sold shells.

_____ Irving decided to find a new home.

_____ Irving found a cracked teacup.

 **Write five sentences telling what you did last Saturday. Be sure to write the events in the order in which they happened. Share your sentences with a family member.**

Name _____ Date _____

Grammar: Irregular Past Tense Verbs

Use with Student Book page 138.

> Irregular verbs do not follow the same rules as regular verbs.
> This chart shows some **irregular past tense verbs.**

Present Tense	Past Tense
grow	grew
fall	fell

A. Write the past tense form of the underlined verb.

1. My dog <u>breaks</u> everything in the room. _____

2. I <u>sleep</u> with the fan on. _____

3. The teacher <u>tells</u> her class a story. _____

4. Mindy <u>goes</u> to Mexico every summer. _____

B. Match each verb with its irregular past tense form. Write the letter of the correct answer.

5. leave _____   **a.** caught

6. swim _____   **b.** swam

7. catch _____   **c.** found

8. find _____   **e.** left

Write one sentence using both forms of the verbs in examples 7 and 8. Show your sentences to a family member.

Spelling: Words with Difficult Spellings

Use with Student Book page 139.

Look at each pair of words. Circle the word that is spelled correctly.

SPELLING TIP

In a notebook, write words you have trouble spelling. Study the words until they become easier to spell.

1. annoy   annoi

2. rok   rock

3. jumped   jumpt

4. tallist   tallest

5. gossip   gossyp

6. dangeris   dangerous

7. nonsense   nonesence

8. leaves   leeves

 Use three of the words to write a short story about an animal that likes to get into mischief.

_____

_____

_____

_____

_____

 **Make a list of three words you want to know how to spell. Work with a family member to find those words in a dictionary to check their spellings.**

Name _____ Date _____

Vocabulary

Use with Student Book pages 140–141.

<table>
<tr><td>

Key Words

fine

whisk

stitches

stroke

bare

wink

</td></tr>
</table>

A. Choose the word that *best* completes each sentence. Write the word.

1. I covered the _____ walls with pictures and photos.

2. My dad smiled proudly and said, "You wrote a

_____ story."

3. When I tell a joke, I _____ and smile.

4. She had only a second to _____ away all the old newspapers.

5. This torn sock just needs a few _____ .

6. Cinderella had to be home at the _____ of midnight.

B. Read each sentence. Circle the word that correctly completes the sentence.

7. This beautiful painting is a (stroke / fine) piece of art.

8. People sometimes (wink / whisk) when they tell a joke.

9. We went to the supermarket because the food cabinet was almost (fine / bare).

10. Just a few more (whisk / stitches) and I'll stop sewing.

Home-School Connection

Choose two key words and show a family member how to find their meanings in a dictionary. Then say a sentence for each word using any of its definitions.

C. Answer the questions.

11. Why does a new house look **bare**?

_____

12. When do you **wink**?

_____

13. Where were you last night at the **stroke** of eight?

_____

14. Why might a person **whisk** something away?

_____

15. When does something need **stitches**?

_____

16. What is something you think is **fine**?

_____

D. Read each question. Write a response using the underlined word.

17. Why is playing baseball a <u>voluntary</u> activity?

_____

18. Why do you <u>appreciate</u> helpful people?

_____

 Write a second answer for each question. Share your answers with a family member.

Name _____ Date _____

Reader's Companion

Use with Student Book pages 142–149.

The Shoemakers and the Elves

Lumkin: Let's play a trick on them!

Pixie: No, Lumkin. I think we have had enough fun for one day. We need a warm place to rest.

Lumkin: You're right. I don't want to get chased out of another house. I'm cold.

Pixie: [She looks in the window again.] Those people look tired.

Lumkin: And their shelves look bare. The shoemakers have nothing to sell.

Use What You Know

List two ways Lumkin and Pixie helped the shoemakers.

1. _____

2. _____

Reading Strategy

MARK the TEXT

Circle the sentence that gives information about what season it might be.

Comprehension Check

MARK the TEXT

The elves say the shoemakers have nothing to sell. Underline the sentence that tells you how they know that.

Use the Strategy

How did making inferences and predictions help you understand this passage?

_____

_____

_____

Retell It!

Retell this passage. Pretend it is a fairy tale. Start with the phrase "Once upon a time…"

_____

_____

_____

_____

Reader's Response

What lesson did you learn from the passage?

_____

_____

_____

Retell the passage to a family member.

Name _____ Date _____

Phonics: Vowel Pair *ea*

Use with Student Book page 150.

> The **vowel pair *ea*** can have two sounds—the long *e* sound, as in *each*, and the short *e* sound, as in *head*.

A. Check the box that tells which vowel sound each word has.

	long e sound	short e sound
1. ready	☐	☐
2. neat	☐	☐
3. mean	☐	☐
4. heavy	☐	☐
5. please	☐	☐

B. Read each clue. Fill in the letters to complete the answer. In the box, write S if the word has the short *e* sound and L if it has the long *e* sound.

6. you need this to make a sandwich   _____ _____ e a _____ ☐

7. birds have these   _____ e a _____ _____ ☐

8. you do this while you sleep   _____ _____ e a _____ ☐

Get a newspaper or magazine article. Underline the words that have the short *e* vowel sound spelled *ea*. Draw a box around the words that have the long *e* vowel sound spelled *ea*. Show your work to a family member.

Comprehension: Infer and Predict

Use with Student Book pages 152–153.

Read the passage. Use what the author has told you to answer the questions. Write a complete sentence for each answer.

The Picnic

Ashley, Tawana, and Gina liked being together. So they planned a weekend picnic. Each girl would bring something on Saturday. They all decided to bring their favorite games.

Ashley wanted to bake an apple pie. Tawana wanted to make a salad. Gina said she would buy lemonade at the store.

On Saturday Ashley looked out the window. Dark clouds were in the sky. Suddenly, the phone rang. It was Tawana. She said, "Ashley, I have some bad news!"

1. How do you know Ashley, Tawana, and Gina are friends?

_____

2. How do you know the girls like to play games?

_____

3. How do you know Ashley and Tawana like to cook?

_____

4. How do you know Saturday's weather is bad?

_____

What will happen the next time the three girls go on a picnic? Write three sentences that show your predictions. Share your sentences with a family member.

Name _____ Date _____

Grammar: The Verb *Have*

Use with Student Book page 154.

> The verb **have** means to own or possess. This chart shows the different forms of the verb in the present tense.

Subject	Form of *have*
he, she, it, Pablo	has
I, you, we, they, people, dogs	have

Complete each sentence with the correct present tense form of *have*.

1. They _____ a new house.

2. It _____ three big bedrooms.

3. Do you _____ any brothers or sisters?

4. Stuart always _____ the best ideas.

5. My mother _____ a great plan.

6. I _____ to speak to you right now!

7. Today we will _____ friends over for dinner.

8. Can we _____ soup for lunch?

9. She _____ to study for school.

10. Donald and Amy _____ a big dog.

Write a paragraph about some of the things that you and your family have. Use the verb *have* at least five times in the paragraph.

77

Spelling: Vowel Pairs with a Long Vowel Sound

Use with Student Book page 155.

Each word below has a long vowel sound spelled *ai, ay, ea,* or *oa*. Add a letter to complete each word. Then write the word.

1. d a _____   _____

2. r _____ a d   _____

3. r a _____ n   _____

4. l _____ a v e   _____

5. s _____ y   _____

6. c l e _____ n   _____

7. p _____ i d   _____

8. t o _____ s t   _____

Use three of the words to write a dialogue between two farm workers.

_____

_____

_____

_____

Home-School Connection Think of two more words for each of the vowel pairs. Use each word in a sentence. Show your sentences to a family member.

Name _____ Date _____

Review

Use with Student Book pages 108–155.

A. Answer the questions after reading Unit 3. You can go back and reread to help find the answers.

1. Which question is NOT answered by the end of *My Museum Friend*? Circle the letter of the correct answer.

    a. Will the dinosaur and his visitor meet again?

    b. Is the dinosaur extinct?

    c. Did his species once roam the Earth?

    d. Are dinosaur fossils found in sandstone?

2. Read these sentences from the poem.

> Extinct! That's what I am to you.   Like a puff of smoke I disappeared.
> My whole world went haywire.   Because of ice, an asteroid, or fire.

    What does *extinct* mean? Circle the letter of the correct answer.

    a. hard   **c.** species

    b. dead   **d.** muscles

3. Write a sentence telling why scientists dig for dinosaur fossils.

_____

4. Think of the sequence of events in *Why Mosquitoes Buzz in People's Ears*. Which sentence is NOT in the correct order? Circle the letter of the correct answer.

    a. Monkey jumped to the highest tree.

    b. One of Owl's eggs fell to the ground.

    c. Lion told Mosquito he can never talk again.

    d. Owl was sad and did not hoot.

5. Why did the animal council meet?

_____

_____

_____

6. Circle the word that does NOT have a long vowel pair.

wait   three   today   friend   toe   fruit

7. Circle the sentence that uses the verb *have* incorrectly.

   a. The elves have an hour to make shoes.

   b. Amelia has to get out of bed early.

   c. Diego haves leather to make shoes.

   d. Pixie and Lumkin have to leave soon.

B. Read the dialogue from *The Shoemakers and the Elves*. Then answer questions 8 and 9.

Dialogue	Infer/Predict
Amelia: Look, Diego! Shoes! I must be dreaming!	**a.** Amelia is angry at Diego.
Diego: Did you get up and work last night?	**b.** Amelia likes the color of the shoes.
Amelia: No! I was going to ask you the same thing!	**c.** Amelia thought Diego made the shoes.
	d. Amelia wants to thank the elves.

8. Draw a box around the word in the dialogue that has a vowel pair with the long e sound.

9. Circle the correct inference.

Tell a family member something new you learned from this unit.

Name _____ Date _____

Vocabulary

Use with Student Book pages 168–169.

Key Words

- salvage
- urban
- rural
- vacant
- creative
- reuse

A. Choose the word that *best* completes each sentence. Write the word.

1. Did they _____ anything from the house that burned?

2. Farms are located in _____ areas.

3. The building is _____. No one lives there.

4. Writers and artists are _____ people.

5. I like to _____ things instead of throwing them out.

B. Unscramble the words. Then write a definition for the word.

6. g l a s a e v _____

_____

7. s u r e e _____

_____

8. b r a u n _____

_____

9. c t v n a a _____

_____

10. r l u a r _____

_____

C. Answer the questions.

11. What might you see in an **urban** area?

_____

12. Why is an artist a **creative** person?

_____

13. Why is it a good idea to **reuse** old things?

_____

14. When does **salvage** work take place?

_____

15. What might you find in a **rural** area?

_____

16. How might you make a **vacant** lot look better?

_____

Academic Words

D. Read each sentence. Write a new sentence using the underlined word.

17. The <u>construction</u> of the new school will take one year.

_____

18. Jim likes my puppy, <u>despite</u> his fear of dogs.

_____

 Think of a second answer for each of the questions. Share your answers with a family member.

Name _____   Date _____

Reader's Companion

Use with Student Book pages 170–173.

New Life for Old Buildings

Not long ago, people tore down old buildings. Usually, they replaced old buildings with new ones. Sometimes they just left empty lots. When these buildings came down, people lost important links to the past.

People have learned that they can use an old building for a new purpose. They are finding creative ways to reuse buildings. Mansions have become museums. Schools have become apartment buildings. Railroad stations have become shopping centers.

Genre

Underline one sentence that tells you *New Life for Old Buildings* is informational text.

Reading Strategy

Circle one sentence that gives an example of a cause and its effect.

Comprehension Check

List three ways to reuse a building.

1. _____

2. _____

3. _____

Use the Strategy

What happens when people tear down an old building? To find the answer, look for cause and effect in the first paragraph.

_____

_____

_____

Retell It!

Retell this passage. Pretend you are the mayor of a town. Tell why you want people to preserve old buildings.

_____

_____

_____

_____

Reader's Response

What old building in your community do you think should be salvaged? How would you reuse the building?

_____

_____

_____

Summarize the passage for a family member.

Name _____ Date _____

Phonics: Digraph *ow*

Use with Student Book page 174.

> The **digraph *ow*** can have the long *o* sound you
> hear in *grow* or the vowel sound you hear in *how*.

**A. Read each sentence. Underline the words with *ow* that have a
long *o* sound. Draw a box around the words with *ow* that have
the vowel sound as in the word *how*.**

1. The clown was in the show.

2. Do you know what town she lives in?

3. Plow trucks come out when it snows.

4. I like red and yellow flowers the best!

5. Will you throw the ball to me now?

B. Write each word in the correct column of the chart.

allow   below   now   slow   throw   towel

ow spells the long *o* sound as in *grow*	*ow* spells the vowel sound as in *how*

**Think of three more examples of *ow* words for each vowel sound.
Show your words to a family member.**

85

Comprehension: Cause and Effect

Use with Student Book pages 176–177.

A. Match each cause with its effect. Write the letter of the correct answer.

Cause	Effect
_____ **1.** We lost power after a big storm.	**a.** We couldn't use the computer.
_____ **2.** My dad got a new job.	**b.** She did well on the test.
_____ **3.** Erin studied every night.	**c.** A police officer had to direct traffic.
_____ **4.** A traffic light broke.	**d.** We moved to another city.

B. Read the passage. Then complete the chart.

Our New House

Mom and Dad saved money for a long time. Finally they could buy a new house. The house was very old. It needed many repairs. There was a lot of work to be done, so everybody had to help. My sister and I painted the kitchen. My brothers planted trees. Now our yard looks like a forest!

Cause	Effect
Mom and Dad saved money.	
	The house needed repairs.
My brothers planted trees.	

Pretend it snowed last night. Write three sentences that explain the snow storm's effect. Show your sentences to a family member.

Name _____ Date _____

Grammar: Adverbs

Use with Student Book page 178.

> **Adverbs** are words that tell about verbs. Adverbs add information and usually tell how something happens.

Underline the adverb in each sentence.

1. She ran quickly down the street.

2. Every morning, the sun shines brightly.

3. Did you work hard on your report?

4. The movie ended sadly.

5. Slowly, he opened the door.

6. I always eat my breakfast.

7. The music played very loudly.

8. Sometimes we swim at the lake.

9. The waves crashed noisily on the beach.

10. Make your bed now!

 **Write five sentences with adverbs. Show your sentences to a family member.**

Spelling: **The /f/ Sound Spelled** *ph*

Use with Student Book page 179.

alphabet	dolphin	elephant
Joseph	nephew	paragraphs

Write each word in the correct category.

Animals	
People	
Things You Learn about in English Class	

Choose one of the categories. Write two sentences using the words from that category.

_____

_____

_____

_____

Write two more words with the /f/ sound spelled *ph*. Show your words to a family member.

Name _____ Date _____

Vocabulary

Use with Student Book pages 180–181.

Key Words

government
candidates
campaign
law
politics
office

A. Match each word with its definition. Write the letter of the correct answer.

1. office _____
2. candidates _____
3. law _____
4. government _____
5. campaign _____
6. politics _____

a. group of people who make laws

b. rules that people have to follow

c. people who want to be elected

d. working to get elected

e. an important position in government

f. activities of people in government

B. Read each sentence. Write TRUE or FALSE.

7. Presidents must campaign to be elected. _____

8. It is against the law to go to school. _____

9. Your state has its own government. _____

10. Any voter can get involved in politics. _____

11. Candidates want to be elected. _____

12. Students cannot run for office in a school election. _____

C. Answer the questions.

13. When do people **campaign**?

_____

14. What do **candidates** do to get elected?

_____

15. Who leads the United States **government**?

_____

16. How do people get involved in **politics**?

_____

17. Why do people obey the **law**?

_____

18. What political **office** would you like to run for?

_____

Academic Words

D. Read each sentence. Write a new sentence using the underlined word.

19. I do my homework to <u>ensure</u> I get good grades.

_____

20. Politicians <u>commit</u> to helping the people.

_____

 **Home-School Connection** Use two vocabulary words to tell a family member what you know about politics.

Name _____ Date _____

Reader's Companion

Use with Student Book pages 182–187.

Running for Office

A life in politics isn't always easy. Candidates need everyone's vote. So they must meet the voters. They greet shoppers at stores and say hello to people on the street. They put advertisements in newspapers. Sometimes, they debate the other candidates. Each person thinks he or she can do the best job. But they have to share their good ideas with voters.

Candidates promise to do what the people want. Then on Election Day, the people vote. Everyone waits to see who wins. It is an exciting time. The winner is happy. He or she can now help their community.

Genre

MARK the TEXT

Underline one sentence that tells you *Running for Office* is informational text.

Comprehension Check

List three things you know about candidates.

1. _____

2. _____

3. _____

Use What You Know

Write one purpose a reader might have for reading this selection.

_____

91

Use the Strategy

What happens on Election Day? Set a purpose for reading, then go back and find the answer.

_____

_____

_____

Retell It!

Retell this passage. Pretend you are a candidate. Describe what you would do to get people to vote for you.

_____

_____

_____

_____

_____

_____

Reader's Response

What are two ways that candidates campaign for office?

_____

_____

_____

Summarize the passage for a family member.

Name _____ Date _____

Phonics: Soft and Hard c

Use with Student Book page 188.

> The letter *c* usually has the soft sound when it is
> followed by *e, i,* or *y,* as in *price.* Otherwise, the
> letter *c* usually has the hard sound as in *carry.*

A. Read each sentence. Underline the words that have the soft /s/
sound spelled *c.* Draw a box around the words that have the
hard /k/ sound spelled *c.*

1. She can skate on ice.

2. The prince danced all night.

3. Who has the loudest voice in class?

4. Our cat was rescued by a fireman.

5. This sentence was written correctly.

B. Write each word in the correct column of the chart.

face   fact   cool   center   policy   candy

Soft *c* as in *mice*	Hard *c* as in *can*

Home-School Connection Think of two more examples of words with a soft *c* as in *mice* and
two with a hard *c* as in *can.* Show your words to a family member.

93

Comprehension: Set a Purpose for Reading

Use with Student Book pages 190–191.

Read the newspaper article. Think about what the title tells you about the article.

Corey Runs for Office

Corey James wants to be the next Student Council President! Every year, Lincoln Middle School has an election. Election Day will be on Tuesday, September 29. Susanna Clemons and Arturo Diaz are also running for the same office. "They are both good candidates," said Corey. "But I have more experience." Last year, Corey was the captain of the baseball team. He also was vice president of his class. "I know how to lead," said Corey. One of Corey's goals is to have a Holiday Fair. Many students like this idea. Maybe Corey will win the election.

Write questions using the 5 W questions. The first one is done for you. Then write the answers next to each question.

Five W Questions	Answers
1. Who is Corey?	
2. What	
3. Where	
4. When	
5. Why	

Pretend you want to be president of your school's Student Council. Write the 5 W questions that ask about you. Show your questions to a family member.

Name _____ Date _____

Grammar: Four Kinds of Sentences

Use with Student Book page 192.

> A **declarative sentence** makes a statement.
> I am working late today.
>
> An **interrogative sentence** asks a question.
> Will you help me?
>
> An **imperative sentence** gives a command.
> Brush your teeth.
>
> An **exclamatory sentence** expresses strong feelings.
> I feel great!

Read each sentence. Write whether it is a declarative, interrogative, imperative, or exclamatory sentence. The first one is done for you.

1. Who is your favorite candidate? _____interrogative_____

2. Vote for me! _____

3. When is Election Day? _____

4. She is the governor of our state. _____

5. I won the election! _____

6. What office are you running for? _____

7. Come with us to the victory party. _____

8. Molly's picture is in the newspaper. _____

Write one example of each of the four kinds of sentences. Show your sentences to a family member.

Spelling: /g/ and /j/ Sounds Spelled *g*

Use with Student Book page 193.

Write the word that matches each clue.
Then circle what sound the letter *g*
makes in each word.

game	giraffe
great	gold
Georgia	

1. very good _____ /g/ sound /j/ sound

2. shiny yellow _____ /g/ sound /j/ sound

3. animal with a long neck _____ /g/ sound /j/ sound

4. something you play _____ /g/ sound /j/ sound

5. state in the South _____ /g/ sound /j/ sound

Use three of the spelling words in sentences.

_____

_____

_____

_____

Home-School Connection Look through the *G*s in the dictionary. Find two words each that begin with
the /g/ and /j/ sounds spelled *g*. Show your words to a family member.

Name _____ Date _____

Vocabulary
Use with Student Book pages 194–195.

Use with Student Book pages 194–195.

Key Words

opportunity
research
fair
attraction
suggested
persuade

A. Choose the word that *best* completes the sentence. Write the word.

1. He tried to _____ us to see the movie.

2. We learned a lot of information from our

   _____ .

3. I got the _____ to ride a pony.

4. The _____ had rides, food, and games.

B. Write the correct word for each sentence.

5. My new job is a great (opportunity / attraction). _____

6. Which books did you use to do your (fair / research)?

   _____

7. You always (suggested / persuade) me to watch silly movies!

   _____

8. The (attraction / opportunity) had bright lights and loud music.

   _____

9. She (persuade / suggested) I wear shorts instead of pants.

   _____

10. Almost every (fair / opportunity) has a roller coaster.

    _____

C. Answer the questions.

11. When has your teacher **suggested** you do something?

_____

12. When have you done **research**?

_____

13. What **attraction** would you like to see or ride?

_____

14. What **opportunity** do you want to have?

_____

15. Why do people like going to a **fair**?

_____

16. How do you **persuade** friends to help you?

_____

Academic Words

D. Read each sentence. Write a new sentence using the underlined word.

17. The new ferris wheel is <u>enormous</u>.

_____

18. I will <u>convince</u> my friends to ride on the ferris wheel.

_____

Use a thesaurus to find synonyms for three of the vocabulary words.

Name _____   Date _____

Reader's Companion

Use with Student Book pages 196–199.

Problems Stop London Eye

by Archie Hurbane

LONDON, ENGLAND, March 2

"Paris built the Eiffel Tower for the 1889 World's Fair," said Ms. DeMayo. "It became a famous symbol of the city. Other cities wanted their own symbol."

"The Eiffel Tower became the world's tallest structure. Then, four years after it was built, Chicago had the next World's Fair," continued Ms. DeMayo.

"Did Chicago build a tower, too?" asked Mr. Moore.

"No, but Chicago had a problem," said Ms. DeMayo. "It needed its own attraction."

She told everyone about George Ferris. "He suggested that the city build a huge wheel. He believed many people would want to ride it."

Use What You Know

List three things you can do at a fair.

1. _____

2. _____

3. _____

Genre

Circle one feature that tells you this selection is a newspaper article.

Comprehension Check

Paris built a structure for its World's Fair. Underline a sentence that tells you the name of this attraction.

Use the Strategy

Paris built the Eiffel Tower. George Ferris wanted Chicago to build a different attraction. Compare and contrast the Eiffel Tower with George Ferris's idea for Chicago.

_____

_____

_____

Retell It!

Retell this passage. Pretend you were visiting the London Eye. Describe the ferris wheel.

_____

_____

_____

_____

Reader's Response

What structure or attraction do you think is the most interesting in the world? Why?

_____

_____

_____

Summarize the passage for a family member.

Name _____ Date _____

Word Analysis: Thesaurus

Use with Student Book page 200.

> A **dictionary** tells the meaning of a word.
> A **thesaurus** lists synonyms for a word, or
> words with similar meanings.

Read the sentence and the definition for each underlined word. Then write the synonym that is closest in meaning to the underlined word.

1. My answer to the last question was <u>wrong</u>. _____

   wrong *adjective* / not correct: *a wrong turn*

   SYNONYMS: **incorrect** / inaccurate, faulty: *an incorrect conclusion*

   bad / below an accepted level: *bad quality*

2. The <u>last</u> bus left at midnight. _____

   last *adjective* / final in a series: *the last stop*

   SYNONYMS: **final** / the end position: *the final station*

   previous / most recent: *previous job*

3. Will you <u>correct</u> this mistake? _____

   correct *verb* / to remove the errors from: *correct the spelling mistakes*

   SYNONYMS: **improve** / to make better: *improve your work habits*

   fix / to make right: *fix a broken bike*

Home-School Connection

Find three synonyms for the word *good*. Look up each word in the dictionary and use it in a sentence. Show your sentences to a family member.

Comprehension: Compare and Contrast

Use with Student Book pages 202–203.

A. Compare and contrast the items. List two ways they are alike. Then list two ways they are different.

1. a house and an apartment building

alike _____

different _____

2. a cookie and a pie

alike _____

different _____

B. Read the travel article. Compare and contrast the two cities.

Two Cities

Chicago and London are big cities. Chicago is in the middle of the United States. It is on the shore of Lake Michigan. London is in England. The Thames River goes through London. There are parks and paths in both cities. But unlike London, Chicago also has beaches on the lake.

_____

_____

_____

_____

Think of two cities you want to visit. Write two sentences that compare the cities. Then write two sentences that contrast the cities. Show your sentences to a family member.

Name _____ Date _____

Grammar: Compound Words

Use with Student Book page 204.

> A **compound word** is a word made by combining two shorter words.
>
> anyone   backyard   townhouse   railroad

A. Read each sentence. Underline the compound word or words.

1. My bedroom is downstairs.

2. Airplanes and motorcycles make lots of noise.

3. Did you leave the newspaper outside?

4. I had eggs and grapefruit for breakfast.

5. We play tag in the summertime.

B. Add a word to make a compound word. Then write the compound word.

6. some _____   _____

7. _____ thing   _____

8. snow _____   _____

9. _____ self   _____

10. back _____   _____

Think of three more compound words and use them in sentences. Share your sentences with a family member.

Spelling: Use a Dictionary

Use with Student Book page 205.

Use the dictionary definitions to answer the questions.

> **cool** /kool/
>
> 1. **adjective** A little bit cold. *The weather will be cool tonight.*
>
> 2. **verb** To lower the temperature of something. *We can't eat the cookies until they cool.*
>
> 3. **adjective** Unfriendly and distant. *Chico gave me a cool look when he heard my news.*

SPELLING TIP

How can you find a word in the dictionary if you don't know how to spell it? Say the word. What is the first sound? Write that letter. Then say the word again, listen to the next sound, and write it down. Soon, you will have enough letters to help you find the word.

1. What does /kool/ tell you? _____

2. How many definitions are given for *cool* when it is used as an

adjective? _____

3. Write the definition of *cool* as a word that refers to temperature.

_____

✎ **Write a short magazine article about an art exhibit. Use two forms of the word *show* in your writing.**

_____

_____

_____

Home-School Connection

Look up the dictionary definitions for the word *research*. Explain how the word was used in the reading. Use two forms of the word in sentences. Share your sentences with a family member.

Name _____ Date _____

Review

Use with Student Book pages 162–205.

Answer the questions after reading Unit 4. You can go back and reread to help find the answers.

1. Which question is not answered by the end of *New Life for Old Buildings*? Circle the letter of the correct answer.

   a. Why do some people want to save old buildings?
   b. Which architect saved Union Station in St. Louis?
   c. Can people reuse old buildings?
   d. Are people finding creative ways to use old buildings?

2. Write a sentence telling why an old building can be a link to our past.

   _____

   _____

3. Underline the sentence that does not have an adverb in it. Circle the letter of the correct answer.

   a. Our art gallery was a private home.
   b. An architect proudly designed a new library.
   c. She worked hard on the new design.
   d. The busy workers happily fixed the building.

4. Write the adverbs that appear in the three other sentences.

   _____

   _____

5. Circle the word that has the hard c sound.

   campaign   change   policy   dance

Read this passage from *Running for Office*. Then answer questions 6 and 7.

> Candidates promise to do what the people want. Then on Election Day, the people vote. Everyone waits to see who wins. It is an exciting time. The winner is happy. He or she can now help their community.

6. Identify the genre of the passage. Circle the letter of the correct answer.

   a. friendly letter   **b.** informational text   **c.** how-to poster

7. Write a compound word that appears in the passage. _____

Read this passage from *Problems Stop London Eye*. Then answer questions 8 and 9.

> The London Eye was opened on New Year's Eve, 1999. It is England's most popular visitor attraction. The Eye is 443 feet high. Every year, about 3.5 million people have the opportunity to ride it. But yesterday, people had to wait.

8. What does *attraction* mean? Circle the letter of the correct answer.

   a. an inventor of a huge wheel   **c.** something interesting to see
   b. a person who is friendly   **d.** a problem to solve

9. Which sentence *best* completes the Cause and Effect Chart?

Cause	Effect
	Chicago wanted an attraction of its own.

   a. Paris built the famous Eiffel Tower.
   b. George Ferris suggested a huge wheel.
   c. People could ride the ferris wheel.
   d. Paris had a World's Fair.

Tell a family member something new you learned from this unit.

106

Name _____   Date _____

Vocabulary

Use with Student Book pages 218–219.

Use with Student Book pages 218–219.

Key Words

native
extreme
architecture
underground
mining
efficient

A. Choose the word that *best* completes each sentence. Write the word.

1. The workers dug a tunnel deep

   _____.

2. Polar bears can live in _____ cold.

3. Workers look for gold when _____.

4. What animals are _____ to your state?

5. I never waste time because I am _____!

6. Beautiful buildings show why _____ is important.

B. Match each word with its definition. Write the letter of the correct answer.

7. native   _____   a. taking things like gold from below the ground

8. underground _____   b. good at not wasting time

9. mining   _____   c. the look of a building

10. efficient   _____   d. not normal or usual

11. architecture _____   e. from a particular place

12. extreme   _____   f. below the surface of the earth

C. Answer the questions.

13. Why do some people build their homes **underground**?

_____

14. What animals are **native** to your community?

_____

15. When are you the *most* **efficient**?

_____

16. Why is **mining** important?

_____

17. How do people protect themselves from **extreme** weather?

_____

18. What do you like about the **architecture** in your community?

_____

Academic Words

D. Read each sentence. Write a new sentence using the underlined word.

19. Cut flowers <u>survive</u> longer when you put them in water.

_____

20. Living in New York City is a <u>unique</u> experience.

_____

 **Define three key words in your own words. Show your definitions to a family member.**

Name _____ Date _____

Reader's Companion

Use with Student Book pages 220–225.

The Underground City

About 3,500 people live in Coober Pedy, Australia. From the street, you might see only dirt and some trees. But under the ground, there are homes! More than half of the people in the town live in underground houses. These are regular houses. They look a lot like yours!

The summer heat in Coober Pedy is extreme. But the underground homes are efficient. They stay cool during the hot months. That means people don't spend money on air conditioning. In the winter, the homes stay warm. That means people pay less for heat.

Use What You Know

List three things you know about Coober Pedy, Australia.

1. _____

2. _____

3. _____

Reading Strategy

MARK the TEXT

Underline one fact from the passage. Circle one opinion from the passage.

Comprehension Check

MARK the TEXT

Put a line through one sentence that explains how Coober Pedy's underground homes are efficient.

Use the Strategy

Find one fact in the first paragraph of the passage. Explain why it is a fact and not an opinion.

_____

_____

_____

Retell It!

Retell this passage. Pretend you want a friend to move to Coober Pedy, Australia.

_____

_____

_____

_____

Reader's Response

Would you like to live in an underground house? Why or why not?

_____

_____

_____

Summarize the passage for a family member.

Name _____ Date _____

Word Analysis: Homophones
Use with Student Book page 226.

> **Homophones** are words that sound the same but have different spellings and meanings.

Read each homophone pair. Then write the word that goes with each sentence.

1. | ate, eight | I _____ breakfast with my dad.

   My brother is _____ years old.

2. | hear, here | Do you live _____ or over there?

   Did you _____ that noise?

3. | sail, sale | She bought a shirt at the _____.

   We _____ our boat on the lake.

4. | flour, flower | My baker needs _____ to make bread.

   Only one _____ bloomed in the garden.

5. | knew, new | There is a _____ student in class.

   Suzanne _____ every answer on the test.

6. | sea, see | They couldn't _____ anything in the dark.

   We traveled by boat across the _____.

Use each of these words in sentences: *to, two, too.* Show your sentences to a family member.

Comprehension: Fact and Opinion

Use with Student Book pages 228–229.

Read each sentence. Write F for fact or O for opinion.

1. Living underground is fun! _____

2. I think everyone in class is nice. _____

3. Mining is dangerous work. _____

4. Most people want to live near the ocean. _____

5. Deserts have extreme weather. _____

6. Everyone in class took the test. _____

7. Summer weather is terrible! _____

8. Kids like going to school every day. _____

9. Many people live near oceans and lakes. _____

10. Some homes are built of wood and stone. _____

Home-School Connection Imagine you live underground. Write one fact and one opinion about living underground. Show your fact and opinion to a family member.

Name _____   Date _____

Grammar: Commas in Place Names and Dates

Use with Student Book page 230.

Rule	Example
Use a comma between the name of a city and its state. Use a comma between the name of a city and its country.	I live in Sacramento, California. She lives in Madrid, Spain.
Use a comma between the day and year. When the date appears in the middle of a sentence, add a comma after the year.	My family came to America on April 23, 2001. On May 3, 2002, I was born.

A. Read the place names and dates. Write YES if a comma is needed. Write NO if a comma is not needed.

1. March 3 1995 _____   **3.** November 12 _____

2. Boston Massachusetts _____   **4.** the city of Sacramento _____

B. Rewrite each sentence. Place a comma in the correct places.

5. Grandma celebrated her birthday on July 25 2007 in Atlanta Georgia.

_____

6. On March 3 2007 I moved to Rome Italy.

_____

7. My parents were married in Chicago on July 1 1989.

_____

Look through a newspaper article for examples of place names and dates. Find three examples that include a comma. Show your work to a family member.

Spelling: /s/ Sound Spelled c

Use with Student Book page 231.

Fill in each blank with a letter to solve the clue.

> ### SPELLING TIP
> When the letter *c* makes the *s* sound, *e*, *i*, or *y* always follows the *c*.

1. frozen water   _____ c e

2. large town   c i _____ _____

3. round shape   c i _____ _____ _____ _____

4. you can ride one   _____ _____ c y _____ _____ _____

5. cats chase them   _____ _____ c e

6. the middle   c e _____ _____ _____ _____

7. coin worth one   c e _____ _____

8. good or friendly   _____ _____ c e

9. your eyes and mouth are on it   _____ _____ c e

10. baby swan   c y _____ _____ _____ _____

 Write sentences using two of the answer words.

_____

_____

_____

_____

Write four more words that have the /s/ sound spelled *c*. Two of the words should begin with the /s/ sound; two of the words should have the /s/ sound. Show your words to a family member.

Name _____ Date _____

Vocabulary

Use with Student Book pages 232–233.

Key Words

- prairie
- sod
- climate
- harsh
- record

A. Choose the word that *best* matches the meaning of the underlined words. Write the word.

1. The <u>usual weather</u> is hot and rainy.

   _____

2. Snow and ice make winters seem <u>extreme</u>. _____

3. Cows spend their days on the <u>very large grasslands</u>.

   _____

4. The <u>thick layer of grass</u> feels soft under our feet. _____

5. The girls kept a <u>written history</u> of their experiences.

   _____

B. Choose the word that *best* completes each sentence. Write the word.

6. Our front yard is covered with thick _____.

7. A report card is a _____ of your grades.

8. Wild animals lived on the _____.

9. It snows a lot in places where the _____ is cold.

10. When the winter weather is _____, I play indoors.

C. Answer the questions.

11. Why is a **prairie** important to animals?

_____

12. What do people keep a **record** of?

_____

13. Where is the weather **harsh?**

_____

14. How do people use **sod?**

_____

15. What is the **climate** like where you live?

_____

Academic Words

D. Read each sentence. Write a new sentence using the underlined word.

16. The forest is home to many <u>domestic</u> animals.

_____

17. If they build houses here, it will <u>alter</u> the land.

_____

Use the key words to tell about life on the prairie.

Name _____ Date _____

Reader's Companion
Use with Student Book pages 234–239.

A House of Grass

Dear Molly,

I have funny news! We live in a sod house! It is dark and damp. But do not worry. It will protect us from the climate. It is an excellent shelter!

There are few trees on the prairie. The land looks like a sea of grass.

Love,

Sarah

Dear Sarah,

I would love to live near you again. But I would not like to live on the frontier! I prefer my life in Boston.

When I look out my window, I see churches, museums, and stores. These are strong buildings. They were built to last forever. But even rain could hurt your buildings. Your house could turn to mud.

A sod house does not appeal to me. I do not like grass or dirt. I do not want to live with bugs!

Love,

Molly

Use What You Know

List three things you know about sod houses.

1. _____
2. _____
3. _____

Reading Strategy

MARK the TEXT

Underline one sentence that tells you why Sarah is writing to Molly.

Comprehension Check

MARK the TEXT

Circle two sentences that tell you why Molly does not want to live on the prairie.

Use the Strategy
Why does Molly write to Sarah?

_____

_____

_____

Retell It!
Retell this passage. Pretend you are Sarah writing to a friend. Describe your new life.

_____

_____

_____

_____

_____

Reader's Response
Would you like to live in a sod house? Why or why not?

_____

_____

_____

Summarize the passage for a family member.

Name _____ Date _____

Phonics: *Y* as a Vowel
Use with Student Book page 240.

> The letter **y** sometimes acts as a vowel.
> - The letter *y* usually has the **long *i* sound** when it comes after a consonant at the end of a one-syllable word.
> - The letter *y* usually has the **long *e* sound** when it comes after a consonant at the end of a word with more than one syllable.

Read each sentence. Underline the word that has the long *e* or long *i* sound spelled *y*. Then circle the correct sound. The first one is done for you.

1. We are moving to the <u>city</u>.   (long *e*)   long *i*

2. You should try to visit us.   long *e*   long *i*

3. The baby will have a big room.   long *e*   long *i*

4. My new room has two closets.   long *e*   long *i*

5. I think I'll be happy in our new house.   long *e*   long *i*

6. The house is large and sunny.   long *e*   long *i*

7. I hope I won't cry when I leave Kansas.   long *e*   long *i*

8. I will miss the beautiful sky!   long *e*   long *i*

Think of two words each with the long *e* and long *i* sounds. Show your words to a family member.

Comprehension: Author's Purpose

Use with Student Book pages 242–243.

Read each sentence to find out if the author's purpose is to entertain, persuade, or inform. The first one is done for you.

1. The winters on the prairie are harsh.

inform

2. You must read this wonderful book.

_____

3. The bugs in sod houses are delicious to eat.

_____

4. The sod on the prairie is very thick.

_____

5. Sod houses look a lot like today's houses.

_____

6. You will love my new home, so please visit.

_____

Write one sentence that compares a sod house to your home. Then write one sentence that contrasts a sod house with your home. Show your sentences to a family member.

Name _____ Date _____

Grammar: Commas in a Series

Use with Student Book page 244.

> **Writers use commas to separate three or more items in a series.**
>
> We visited Utah, Idaho, and Nevada.

Rewrite each sentence using commas to separate items in a series.

1. Mom and Dad traveled through mountains deserts and prairies.

_____

2. Sod houses igloos and log cabins are three kinds of homes.

_____

3. On Saturday we shopped played baseball and went swimming.

_____

4. The land was hot dry and dusty.

_____

5. Florida Georgia Alabama and Texas are in the South.

_____

6. We ate breakfast lunch and dinner on the back porch.

_____

Home-School Connection Write two sentences that use commas in a series. Share your sentences with a family member.

Spelling: Adding -er or -r to mean "more"

Use with Student Book page 245.

Read each sentence. Write the word that means the same thing as the words in parentheses. The first one is done for you.

> **SPELLING TIP**
>
> Add -er to a word to mean "more." When a word ends in silent e, you only need to add -r.

1. Winters were _____harsher_____ on
   (more harsh)
   the prairie.

2. Cats are _____ than lions.
   (more small)

3. The trip took _____ than we thought.
   (more long)

4. A brick house is _____ than a sod house.
   (more strong)

5. Last week, the weather was _____.
   (more nice)

6. I think the grass is _____ in Kansas.
   (more green)

7. This apple is _____ than that one.
   (more ripe)

8. Which animal do you think is _____?
   (more smart)

9. It's much _____ in the forest.
   (more cold)

 **Home-School Connection** Write a new sentence for each of the spelling words. Show your sentences to a family member.

Name _____ Date _____

Vocabulary
Use with Student Book pages 246–247.

Key Words

nest
amenities
comforts
structures
natural

A. Read each clue. Unscramble the letters to write the word that matches the clue.

1. things that make a hotel stay pleasant

   m i i a t n e e s _____

2. to get comfortable

   s e t n _____

3. things that make you feel nice and relaxed

   o f m t o c s r _____

4. buildings

   c u t s s r r t e u _____

5. things that come from the world around us

   t a r a n u l _____

B. Read each sentence. Write TRUE or FALSE.

6. People build structures. _____

7. Plastic is a natural material. _____

8. Birds like to nest in trees. _____

9. Travelers never miss the comforts of home. _____

10. Running water and heat are two basic amenities. _____

C. Answer the questions.

11. What are some **structures** that people build?

_____

12. Why do birds like to **nest** high in the trees?

_____

13. What special **comforts** are found in your home?

_____

14. Why do some people use **natural** materials to build their houses?

_____

15. What **amenities** do you find in many hotels?

_____

Academic Words

D. Read each sentence. Write a new sentence using the underlined word.

16. The hotel can <u>accommodate</u> many visitors.

_____

17. The mayor showed us the <u>design</u> for the new school.

_____

 Pretend you live in a treehouse. List three amenities you would like to have. Show your list to a family member.

Name _____ Date _____

Reader's Companion

Use with Student Book pages 248–251.

Living in the Trees

Most of us know what treehouses are. Usually they are simple structures built in trees. They are made by securing a few wood boards to strong tree branches. You climb trees or ladders to get to them.

This kind of treehouse is found in many backyards. Perhaps you have even been in one.

Treehouses are fun places for play or rest. But would you want to live in one? Lots of people do!

Use What You Know

List three things you know about treehouses.

1. _____

2. _____

3. _____

Reading Strategy

Circle one sentence that helps you visualize what a treehouse looks like.

Comprehension Check

Put a line through the sentence that explains what a treehouse is.

Use the Strategy

To get to a treehouse, you need to climb a ladder. Tell what a treehouse looks like to someone on the ground.

_____

_____

_____

Retell It!

Retell this passage. Pretend you are visiting a treehouse. Tell a friend what it is like.

_____

_____

_____

_____

_____

Reader's Response

Would you like to live in a treehouse? Why or why not?

_____

_____

_____

Summarize the passage for a family member.

126

Name _____ Date _____

Phonics: *R-Controlled ar, or, ore*

Use with Student Book page 252.

The letter *r* changes the vowel sound.

| am | ton | toe |
| arm | torn | tore |

Read each sentence. Underline the words with the letters *ar* that have the same vowel sound as in *art*. Draw a box around the words with the letters *or* or *ore* that have the same vowel sound as in *torn* and *tore*.

1. How far is it to the store?

2. We are growing corn in our garden.

3. Every March we go to the shore.

4. The story was hard to read.

5. The pencil is sharp and costs forty cents.

6. We gave Renata a gift and a card for her birthday.

7. Did you come by car or bus?

8. They went to the park yesterday morning.

9. I tore my shirt in the backyard.

10. The pitcher's arm was sore.

Home-School Connection

Write two more words that have the vowel sound *ar* as in *march* and two that have the *or/ore* sound as in *torn* and *tore*. Show your words to a family member.

127

Comprehension: Visualize

Use with Student Book pages 254–255.

Read each paragraph. Write words that helped you to visualize each scene.

1. It was a windy day. Sand blew into my face. Up in the sky, a blue kite danced in the wind. Suddenly, my big umbrella flew into the water.

_____

2. Something was wrong. First the washing machine moved back and forth. Then it began to shake. Suddenly, the top popped open. Water spilled onto the floor. "What a mess!" Kelly thought.

_____

3. The windows were broken. The front door made a loud noise when it opened. The paint was falling off the walls. My grandparents had used the barn to keep chickens. But now we use it as a playhouse.

_____

4. It snowed for two days. The town was buried under snow. Amos stayed inside. He walked over to the window. It was covered in ice.

_____

 **Tell a family member a fairy tale. Use words that will help the family member visualize the subject.**

Name _____ Date _____

Grammar: Adjectives and Articles

Use with Student Book page 256.

> **Adjectives** describe nouns. **Articles** point out nouns.
> We climbed the tall tree.
>
> tall is an adjective   the is an article

A. Read each sentence. Underline each adjective. Draw a box around each article.

1. The treehouse is a fun place to play.

2. We built it on the strongest tree limbs.

3. Mom used a saw to cut the smaller branches.

4. Dad had a treehouse when he was a little boy.

5. I'm a lucky guy!

B. Rewrite each sentence using the correct article. Write the article *a* before words that begin with a consonant. Write the article *an* before words that begin with a vowel.

6. Last summer, I had _____ adventure.

7. I got _____ tent for my birthday.

8. Then my dad took me on _____ camping trip.

9. We stayed near _____ old fort.

10. It had _____ big wall around it.

Write a short paragraph about an adventure you had. Include at least two articles and two adjectives in your writing. Show your paragraph to a family member.

Spelling: Syllables

Use with Student Book page 257.

Spell each of the words below by dividing it into syllables. The first one is done for you.

SPELLING
TIP

Divide a word into syllables to help you spell it.

1. protect   pro tect

2. structures   _____

3. treehouse   _____

4. generations   _____

5. amenities   _____

6. natural   _____

7. accommodate   _____

8. dangerous   _____

9. architecture   _____

10. backyards   _____

Use three of the words to write a paragraph about a house.

_____

_____

_____

Choose any five words. Say them aloud to a family member. Write the words by dividing them into syllables.

Name _____   Date _____

Review

Use with Student Book pages 212–257.

Answer the questions after reading Unit 5. You can go back and reread to help find the answers.

1. Which question is NOT answered by the end of *The Underground City?* Circle the letter of the correct answer.

   a. How many people live in Coober Pedy?
   b. Are the underground houses warm in the winter?
   c. Why do people want to live in caves?
   d. Are opals native to Coober Pedy?

2. Read the sentences. Circle the two homophones.

   > It would be nice to visit Coober Pedy. Many of the houses are unusual. They are not made of wood or brick. They are in caves underground.

3. Read the sentence. Write **F** for fact or **O** for opinion.

   Many people in Coober Pedy live in caves. _____

4. Which sentence needs a comma? Circle the letter of the correct answer.

   a. Have you been to Coober Pedy?
   b. It is a small town in Australia.
   c. It reminded me of Tucson, Arizona.
   d. My grandfather first visited the town on January 26 1965.

5. Circle the word that does not use *y* as a vowel.

   yellow   story   sorry   try

Read this passage from *A House of Grass*. Then answer questions 6 and 7.

> Dear Molly,
>
> I have funny news! We live in a sod house! It is dark and damp. But do not worry. It will protect us from the climate. It is an excellent shelter!
>
> Love,
> Sarah

6. Identify the genre of the passage.

    a. friendly letter   **b.** informational text   **c.** how-to poster

7. Does Sarah like her new home on the prairie? How do you know?

_____

_____

8. Which sentence helps you to visualize a treehouse? Circle the letter of the correct answer.

    a. Most of us know what treehouses are.
    b. A treehouse can be a real home.
    c. Like birds, treehouse dwellers have a happy home in the trees.
    d. Many people around the world live in treehouses.

9. Write the article that appears in sentence d.

_____

Tell a family member something new you learned from this unit.

Name _____ Date _____

Vocabulary

Use with Student Book pages 270–271.

Use with Student Book pages 270–271.

Key Words

signatures

mission

astronaut

plaque

explorer

surrounded

A. Choose the word that _best_ completes each sentence. Write the word.

1. The crew's _____ was to reach the moon.

2. A safe campfire is _____ by stones.

3. Each winner's name is on the _____ .

4. My friends put their _____ on my birthday card.

5. Ernest Shackleton was the first _____ to reach the South Pole.

6. An _____ named Neil Armstrong walked on the Moon.

B. Match each word with its definition. Write the letter of the correct answer.

7. astronaut   _____   **a.** to be all around something

8. surrounded   _____   **b.** person who travels to an unknown place

9. signatures   _____   **c.** person who flies into space

10. plaque   _____   **d.** metal or stone with writing on it

11. explorer   _____   **e.** a group's goal or plan

12. mission   _____   **f.** names written on a piece of paper

C. Answer the questions.

13. Where might an **astronaut** go in the future?

_____

14. Why might someone receive a **plaque**?

_____

15. What **explorer** would you like to learn more about?

_____

16. Where do people write their **signatures**?

_____

17. What plants **surrounded** a house or building you have seen?

_____

18. What might scientists learn on a **mission** to Mars?

_____

Academic Words

D. Read each sentence. Write a **new sentence** using the underlined word.

19. When did the accident <u>occur</u>?

_____

20. I can <u>justify</u> spending my money on a good book.

_____

 Draw pictures to illustrate two key words. Label each picture with the word. Show your pictures to a family member.

Name _____ Date _____

Reader's Companion

Use with Student Book pages 272–279.

The Moon Tree

They called themselves the Moon Tree Crew. Then Stuart named the tree. He said, "Our moon tree needs a name. People will care more about a tree called . . . Apollo."

Stuart knew about these things. His father worked in the advertising business.

Mrs. Wu made posters. Each poster had a slogan: "Save Apollo, the moon tree."

The boys and their friends were busy. Some went to stores. Others walked down Main Street. They told people the moon tree's story. The whole town wanted to help. The Moon Tree Crew got hundreds of signatures.

Use What You Know

List three things you would like to save.

1. _____

2. _____

3. _____

Comprehension Check

The special tree is going to be cut down. Draw a line through one sentence that tells what the boys do to solve this problem.

MARK the TEXT

Genre

MARK the TEXT

Underline one sentence that tells you *The Moon Tree* is realistic fiction.

135

Use the Strategy

Mrs. Wu and the boys had a problem. They wanted to get people to care about the moon tree. What was their solution?

_____

_____

_____

Retell It!

Retell the passage. Pretend you are Stuart or Hector and you just found the moon tree.

_____

_____

_____

_____

_____

Reader's Response

How else could Hector and Stuart have saved the tree?

_____

_____

_____

Retell the passage to a family member.

Name _____ Date _____

Phonics: Diphthongs *ow* and *ou*

Use with Student Book page 280.

> The letters *ow* and *ou* have the vowel sound you hear in *how* and *loud*.
>
> The letters *ow* can also have the long *o* sound you hear in *low*.

A. Read each sentence. Underline the words with *ow* that have the long *o* sound as in *low*. Draw a box around the words with *ow* or *ou* that have the vowel sound as in *plow* and *loud*.

1. Flowers need water to grow.

2. The brown cow walked slowly across the field.

3. Show me your new house.

4. What sound does an owl make?

B. Write each word in the correct column.

below   blow   cloud   down   glow   town

ow as in *low*	*ow* as in *plow*; *ou* as in *round*

Write two words for each of the spelling/sound patterns. Show your words to a family member.

Comprehension: Problem and Solution

Use with Student Book pages 282–283.

Read the passage. Then fill in the Problem and Solution Chart.

Our Park

My friends and I often took the bus to the park. But it was far away. One day, I had an idea. "Let's make our own park. We can use the vacant lot."

"It's filled with trash," said Jessie.

"There are no trees," said Yolanda.

I smiled. "We have lots of work to do!"

We cleaned the lot. We threw away the garbage.

"Something is missing," said Jessie.

"It's not very pretty," said Yolanda.

They were right. We needed some plants. The next day, Mom bought flowers and bushes. Finally, the lot looked like a park.

"All we need now is a place to sit," I said to Mom.

The next day, Dad bought a picnic table and chairs.

"Our park is nicer than a vacant lot," we said.

Problem	Solution
	The kids take the bus to the park.
The vacant lot is dirty.	
	The kids plant flowers and bushes in the park.
There is no place to sit.	

Home-School Connection Write a paragraph about a problem you had and how you solved the problem. Show your paragraph to a family member.

Name _____ Date _____

Grammar: The Verbs *Be* and *Go*

Use with Student Book page 284.

> ***Be*** and ***go*** are both irregular verbs. You do not form the past tense by adding *-ed*.

A. Read each sentence. Underline the verb. Then write if the verb is the past tense or present tense of the verb *be* or *go*. The first one is done for you.

1. Our family <u>went</u> on a picnic.   past tense of go

2. I am late for class. _____

3. She goes to the store every Friday. _____

4. My neighbor was not home. _____

5. They are in the backyard. _____

B. Complete each sentence. Use the verb and tense shown in parentheses. The first one is done for you.

6. They _____ are _____ in the park. (present tense of *be*)

7. The children _____ to school every day. (present tense of *go*)

8. She _____ your best friend. (present tense of *be*)

9. We _____ to a movie. (past tense of *go*)

10. David _____ at the party. (past tense of *be*)

 Write a short paragraph describing your week. Use at least two different forms of the verb *be* and two different forms of the verb *go*.

139

Spelling: Silent *gh*

Use with Student Book page 285.

Read each clue. Spell a word with silent *gh* to solve each clue.

SPELLING TIP

The letters *gh* are sometimes silent. Notice words with silent *gh* and learn their spellings.

1. opposite of *low*

   _____

2. another word for *correct* _____

3. number between seven and nine _____

4. opposite of *dark* _____

5. very shiny _____

6. how tall you are _____

7. opposite of *day* _____

8. how heavy you are _____

Write a paragraph about yourself. Use three of the answer words.

_____

_____

_____

_____

_____

Home-School Connection Write four more words with the silent *gh*. Show your words to a family member.

Name _____ Date _____

Vocabulary

Use with Student Book pages 286–287.

Use with Student Book pages 286–287.

A. Choose the word that *best* completes each sentence. Write the word.

Key Words

- pride
- objects
- valuable
- memories
- treasures
- roam

1. The artist showed her painting with great

   _____ .

2. All of the useful _____ were placed on a shelf.

3. We watched the animals _____ the plains.

4. My most important _____ are safe in their hiding place.

5. I have many _____ of when I was a small child.

6. The diamond ring is very _____ .

B. Write the word that matches the clue.

7. very important or worth a lot of money   _____

8. to move around an area with no special purpose

   _____

9. events that a person can remember   _____

10. items that can be seen or touched   _____

11. special items that a person keeps   _____

12. to feel good about yourself   _____

C. **Answer the questions.**

13. What **objects** do you see around you?

_____

14. Where do animals **roam**?

_____

15. What is one of your favorite **memories**?

_____

16. When do you have a feeling of **pride** in yourself?

_____

17. Where do people keep **valuable** things?

_____

18. What kinds of **treasures** might you find in a castle?

_____

Academic Words

D. **Read each sentence. Write a new sentence using the underlined word.**

19. The car lights did not work, but Mr. Singh was <u>aware</u> of the problem.

_____

20. Martin had to <u>reject</u> the coach's offer to join the team.

_____

Ask a family member to share his or her favorite school memory. Then tell your favorite school memory. List two ways your school memories are different and two ways they are similar.

Name _____ Date _____

Reader's Companion
Use with Student Book pages 288–291.

Life on the Frontier

Sung to the tune of "Yankee Doodle Dandy"

I came with valuable objects:
Tools, Ma's books, and our dog, Sam.
Now I have some brand new treasures.
One's the farmland I roam
With my new sister, Pam.

It isn't all work and no fun, though.
Pa likes to play his banjo.
Ma will sing. I'll dance a jig.
And little Pam will smile.
We're happy in our new frontier home.

Use What You Know

List three things you know about the frontier.

1. _____
2. _____
3. _____

Comprehension Check

Underline two things the family members took with them to the frontier.

MARK the TEXT

Genre

MARK the TEXT

Circle part of the text that tells you *Life on the Frontier* is a song.

Use the Strategy

Describe what the family does in their new frontier home.

_____

_____

_____

Retell It!

Retell the passage. Pretend it is your story and that you moved to the frontier.

_____

_____

_____

_____

_____

Reader's Response

Would you like to be part of the pioneer family described in the passage? Why or why not?

_____

_____

_____

Sing or retell the song to a family member.

Name _____ Date _____

Word Analysis: Compound Words

Use with Student Book page 292.

> Sometimes two words come together to form a new
> word. These new words are called **compound words**.

A. Underline the compound word in each sentence.
   Then write the smaller words found in it.

1. We had a campfire every night. _____ _____

2. Sometimes the evening breeze was cool. _____ _____

3. Our tent got wet during a thunderstorm. _____ _____

4. I left my notebook at the train station. _____ _____

5. Can we travel on an airplane next summer?

_____ _____

B. Use each word to form a compound word.

box	glasses	rain	thing	tub

6. bath_____

7. _____coat

8. eye_____

9. tool_____

10. any_____

Write as many compound words using the word *sun* as you can.
Show your words to a family member.

145

Comprehension: Summarize

Use with Student Book pages 294–295.

Read the poem. Then answer the questions.

The Pioneers

Across the plains
And over the hills
They traveled
Long ago

In search of land
And open fields
In places
They did not know.

From east to west
On horses and wagons
With dreams
And great hopes, too

The story of
The pioneers
Pleases
Both me and you.

1. Who is the poem about?

_____

2. What did they do?

_____

3. Where did they go?

_____

4. When did they do it?

_____

5. Why did they go?

_____

Think of a poem you have read. Summarize that poem for a family member.

Name _____ Date _____

Grammar: Possessive Nouns and Adjectives

Use with Student Book page 296.

Showing Ownership with Nouns			
Possessive Nouns		Possessive Adjectives	
Singular	Plural	Singular	Plural
brother's, Bob's	*girls', students'*	*my, your, his*	*our, your, their*

Write if the underlined word is a possessive noun or adjective. Write S for singular or P for plural. The first one is done for you.

1. He played his <u>father's</u> banjo.

      possessive noun   S

2. Where is <u>your</u> neighbor from?

_____ _____

3. The <u>astronauts'</u> mission was over.

_____ _____

4. <u>Their</u> older sister bought a new car.

_____ _____

5. I have good memories of <u>our</u> vacation together.

_____ _____

6. We used the <u>explorer's</u> map from long ago.

_____ _____

Find five sentences in a magazine or newspaper that have possessive nouns or possessive pronouns.

Spelling: The /j/ Sound

Use with Student Book page 297.

A. Read each clue. Write the word that matches the clue.

bridge	cages	garage
huge	orange	page

1. you turn it in a book

_____

2. zoo animals live in these

_____

3. this word names a color and a fruit _____

4. another word for *big* _____

5. a car drives over it to cross a river _____

6. place where you park a car _____

B. Write about a place you visited. Use at least two answer words.

_____

_____

_____

_____

Home-School Connection

Think of four more words with the /j/ sound spelled -*ge* and -*dge*.
Write a sentence using each word. Tell a family member your sentences.

Name _____ Date _____

Vocabulary

Use with Student Book pages 298–299.

A. **Read each clue. Underline the key word in the row of letters. Then write the word.**

1. to grow quickly or be in good health   dlelthrivekdge   _____

2. taking a long walk through the woods   triehikingonh   _____

3. full of excitement   sluiwthrillingc   _____

4. land at the bottom of hills   rtcanyonpibs   _____

5. paths or walkways   dilztrailsjafve   _____

B. **Read each sentence. Write TRUE or FALSE.**

6. Amusement park rides can be thrilling. _____

7. A canyon is at the top of a hill. _____

8. Standing on a ledge can be dangerous. _____

9. Plants thrive when it rains often. _____

10. Hiking trails are found in trees. _____

Home-School Connection Ask a family member to help you write ten singular nouns. Then write the plural form of each one.

149

C. Answer the questions.

11. Why do some people like to go **hiking**?

_____

12. What is the most **thrilling** thing that has ever happened to you?

_____

13. Where might **trails** lead?

_____

14. How might a person reach the bottom of a **canyon**?

_____

15. When do crops **thrive**?

_____

16. What might you see if you were standing on a mountain **ledge**?

_____

Academic Words

D. Read each sentence. Write a new sentence using the underlined word.

17. The police tried to <u>pursue</u> the robber.

_____

18. Mom wants to move to a different <u>area</u> of our town.

_____

 Use the key words to tell a story about a unicorn that lives on the side of a mountain. Tell your story to a family member.

Name _____ Date _____

Reader's Companion

Use with Student Book pages 300–307.

A Hike Back in Time

We heard the faint sound of water in the distance. As we walked, the noise got louder. The air felt cooler. Then we turned a corner, and the trail stopped. I saw a tall waterfall pouring into a clear pool.

"Mooney Falls!" I cried.

I glanced at my grandmother's picture. "It looks just like it did fifty years ago."

I dipped my hand into the cool water and let it pour through my fingers. I wondered if my grandmother had done the same thing.

"We should go back," Dad said. "But first, we need a picture."

I stood in front of the waterfall while Dad pulled the camera out of his bag.

"Wait a second," Mom said. She picked up a stick from the side of the trail. "You need a walking stick. Now, you look just like your grandmother."

I looked at the picture again and then held it up. "Grandmother and I are visiting the waterfall together!"

Use What You Know

List three things you know about waterfalls.

1. _____

2. _____

3. _____

Genre

Underline one sentence that tells you *A Hike Back in Time* is realistic fiction.

Reading Strategy

Circle two sentences that tell you something about the setting.

Use the Strategy

The girl says, "Grandmother and I are visiting the waterfall together!" What does she mean?

_____

_____

_____

Retell It!

Retell this passage. List in order three of the things the family heard and saw.

_____

_____

_____

_____

Reader's Response

What older friend or family member is special to you? Why?

_____

_____

_____

Home-School Connection   Retell the passage to a family member.

Name _____ Date _____

Phonics: Variant Vowel *oo*

Use with Student Book page 308.

> Sometimes the letters *oo* have the sound you hear in *took*.
> Sometimes the letters *oo* have the sound you hear in *soon*.

A. Read each sentence. Underline the words with *oo* that have the sound you hear in *took*. Draw a box around the words with *oo* that have the sound you hear in *soon*.

1. Did you have a good time at school today?

2. My wool coat has a hood.

3. The goose ran into the woods.

4. Look at the bright moon!

5. Noodles are my favorite food.

6. Yesterday afternoon we baked cookies.

B. Write each word in the correct column.

book   cool   hook   room

oo as in *too*	*oo* as in *took*

Home-School Connection Add two words to each column of the chart. Show the chart to a family member.

Comprehension: Plot and Setting

Use with Student Book pages 310–311.

Read the passage. Then fill in the chart.

My Name Is Filbert

The Chang family walked along the beach in Cape Cod. The beaches of Cape Cod are beautiful. Shells and colored rocks glow in the sun. Usually, the Changs saw birds and crabs on their walks. But one day, they saw a puppy sitting in the sand.

"I think it's lost," said Mrs. Chang.

Jimmy pointed to the dog's neck. "Look," he said. "It has a dog tag." Mr. Chang read the dog tag. "My name is Filbert." There was a phone number on the tag.

Mrs. Chang reached into her pocket. She pulled out her phone. Soon, two small children and their father came running towards the beach. "Filbert!" they shouted. "Where have you been?"

Filbert ran toward them.

"Thank you!" said the man. "We were very worried about our new puppy!"

Setting	**1.** Where are the Changs? _____
	2. What is it like there? _____
Plot	**3.** What happens first? _____
	4. What happens next? _____
	5. What happens at the end? _____

 **Imagine the story continued. Tell a family member two more things that could happen.**

Name _____ Date _____

Grammar: Quotation Marks

Use with Student Book page 312.

> **Quotation marks** are used around a speaker's exact words.
>   "What are you doing?" she asked.
>   "I am going to the mountains," he said.
>   Eileen asked, "Can I come, too?"

Rewrite each sentence. Add quotation marks and other punctuation where they belong.

1. This is a long trail he said.

_____

2. The guide asked Is this your first visit?

_____

3. Renee said The Grand Canyon is beautiful!

_____

4. Look over here shouted Gerry.

_____

5. Did you see the waterfall asked Margot.

_____

6. My feet hurt I said.

_____

Write a paragraph about a recent conversation you had with a friend. Use quotation marks and capital letters. Show a family member your paragraph.

Spelling: Homophones

Use with Student Book page 313.

Read the sentences that follow *a* and *b*. Then write the homophone that completes the sentences. The first one is done for you.

1. **a.** Do you know the

    _____ *way* _____ to school? I'm lost!

    b. Your puppy is getting really big! How much does he

    _____ *weigh* _____ ?

2. **a.** I did well on the test. All of my answers were

    _____ !

    b. Did you _____ your name at the top of the page?

3. **a.** It's such a hot day! The _____ is so bright!

    b. My _____ is five years old. He calls me Daddy.

4. **a.** What do you want to _____ when you grow up?

    b. Have you ever been stung by a _____ ?

Look up the dictionary definitions for *peace/piece* and *great/grate*. Then use each word in a sentence. Share your sentences with a family member.

156

Name _____ Date _____

Review

Use with Student Book pages 264–313.

Answer the questions after reading Unit 6. You can go back and reread to help find the answers.

1. Which question is not answered by the end of *The Moon Tree*? Circle the letter of the correct answer.

   a. Who are the Moon Tree Crew?

   b. How does Mrs. Wu help Hector and Stuart?

   c. Does Mr. Bowman spare the tree?

   d. Why do people sign the petition?

2. Read these sentences from the story.

   > Hector held up a paper. "This is a petition," he said. "It says, 'The moon tree is an important part of history. It is too valuable to lose. Please spare our moon tree.' We need everybody in town to sign this petition."

   What does *petition* mean?

   a. signature   **c.** written request

   b. save   **d.** valuable

3. Mr. Bowman wants to build a shopping mall. Why is that a problem for Hector and Stuart?

   _____

4. Which underlined word does NOT have the *o* sound you hear in *loud*? Circle the letter of the correct answer.

   a. Hector <u>found</u> the ball next to a strange, flat stone.

   b. Hector ran to get Stuart <u>without</u> noticing the red flags.

   c. Hector and Stuart knew <u>how</u> to save the moon tree.

   d. Mrs. Wu said that the <u>woods</u> would be gone soon.

157

5. Circle the sentence that does NOT belong in a summary of the poem *Life on the Frontier*.

    a. A family moves from Pennsylvania to Oregon.
    b. They come with some valuable objects.
    c. They rise at dawn and do the chores.
    d. The family grows corn on the farmland.

6. There is a compound word in one of the answers to Question 5. Write the compound word.

_____

7. What is the setting of *Life on the Frontier*?

    a. Pennsylvania   **c.** a city
    b. the frontier   **d.** a music show

8. Read this sentence from *A Hike Back in Time*. Rewrite the sentence adding the correct quotation marks and punctuation.

> I wonder if that's the trail to the waterfall I said to my parents.

_____

9. Read these sentences from *A Hike Back in Time*. Circle the word with the letters *oo* that has the sound you hear in *took*.

>   I dipped my hand into the cool water and let it pour through my fingers.
>   I stood in front of the waterfall while Dad pulled the camera out of his bag.

Home-School Connection Tell a family member something new you learned from this unit.